ÉDITRICE : Caty Bérubé

AUTEURE : Sabrina Thériault

CHARGÉE DE CONTENU : Lauréanne Hallé

CHEF D'ÉQUIPE PRODUCTION ÉDITORIALE : Crystel Jobin-Gagnon

COORDONNATRICE À LA PRODUCTION : Marjorie Lajoie

CHEFS CUISINIERS : Benoit Boudreau (chef d'équipe), Éric Dacier et Richard Houde.

RÉDACTRICE : Raphaële St-Laurent Pelletier

RÉVISEURES : Edmonde Barry, Marie-Christine Bédard, Marilou Cloutier (chef d'équipe rédaction et révision) et Viviane St-Arnaud.

ASSISTANTES À LA PRODUCTION : Sarah Beauregard et Nancy Morel.

CHEF D'ÉQUIPE PRODUCTION GRAPHIQUE : Marie-Christine Langlois

CONCEPTRICES GRAPHIQUES : Sonia Barbeau, Sheila Basque, Annie Gauthier, Marie-Chloë G. Barrette, Karyne Ouellet et Josée Poulin.

STYLISTES CULINAIRES : Laurie Collin, Maude Grimard, Carly Harvey et Christine Morin (chef d'équipe).

PHOTOGRAPHES : Mélanie Blais, Jean-Christophe Blanchet (chef d'équipe par intérim), Michaël Fournier et Rémy Germain.

PHOTOGRAPHES ET VIDÉASTES : Tony Davidson et Francis Gauthier.

SPÉCIALISTE EN TRAITEMENT D'IMAGES ET CALIBRATION PHOTO : Yves Vaillancourt

COLLABORATRICES : Alex Gauvin et Catherine Pelletier.

DIRECTEUR DE LA DISTRIBUTION : Marcel Bernatchez

DISTRIBUTION : Pratico-Pratiques inc. et Messageries ADP.

IMPRESSION : TC Interglobe

Catalogage avant publication de Bibliothèque et Archives nationales du Québec et Bibliothèque et Archives Canada

Titre : Miss Conserves : mes secrets et mes 85 meilleures recettes / Sabrina Thériault.

Noms : Thériault, Sabrina, 1982- auteur.

Description : Comprend des références bibliographiques et un index.

Identifiants : Canadiana 20200082272 | ISBN 9782896588671

Vedettes-matière : RVM : Conservation et mise en conserves. | RVMGF : Livres de cuisine.

Classification : LCC TX603.T54 2020 | CDD 641.4/2–dc23

DÉPÔT LÉGAL : 3e trimestre 2020
Bibliothèque et Archives nationales du Québec
Bibliothèque et Archives Canada
ISBN 9782896588671

Gouvernement du Québec. Programme de crédit d'impôt pour l'édition de livres – Gestion SODEC

PRATICO ÉDITION

7710, boulevard Wilfrid-Hamel, Québec (QC) G2G 2J5
Tél. : 418 877-0259
Sans frais : 1 866 882-0091
Téléc. : 418 780-1716
www.pratico-pratiques.com

Commentaires et suggestions : info@pratico-pratiques.com

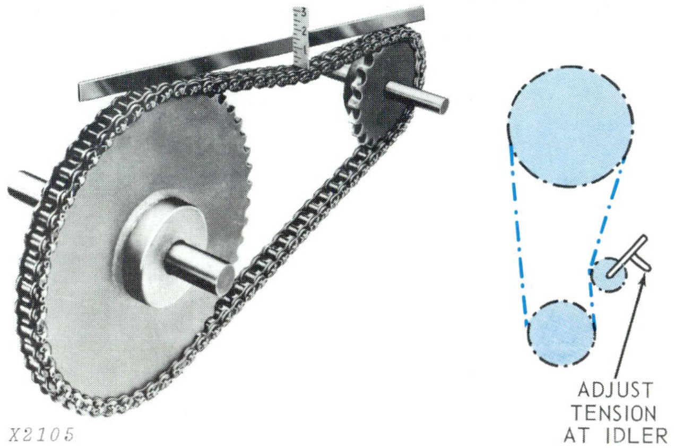

Fig. 24—Checking Tension On Chain

To determine the amount of sag, pull one side of the chain taut, allowing all the excess chain to accumulate in the opposite span.

Place a straight edge over the slack span and pull the chain down at the center (Fig. 24). Measure the amount of sag from the top of the chain to the underside of the straight edge.

If necessary, adjust the shaft centers to provide the recommended amount of sag for proper chain tension.

Stretched Chains

When the shaft or chain tensioner has reached maximum adjustment and the chain begins to ride on the tips of the sprocket teeth (Fig. 25) it may have reached the end of its useful life.

However, if the chain still fits properly when wrapped on the largest sprocket, remove one or two links and reset the shafts or tensioner in their original position. Then adjust to provide proper tension.

LUBRICATION OF CHAIN DRIVES

The importance of lubrication increases with higher chain speeds.

Lubrication will do three basic things for chain life:

1) Reduce wear.

2) Protect against corrosion.

3) Prevent galling or seizing of pins and bushings.

Types Of Lubrication

MANUAL LUBRICATION—Oil is applied with a brush or spout can, preferably once every eight hours of operation and under all conditions. Do this while the chain is still warm. Apply oil again before oil discolors between joints.

DRIP LUBRICATION—Oil drops are directed between the link plate edges from a drip lubricator. Oiling should be sufficient to prevent discoloration of oil between joints.

BATH OR DISK LUBRICATION—With bath lubrication, the lower strand of chain runs through a sump of oil in the drive housing. The oil level should reach the pitch line of the chain at its lowest operating level. With disk lubrication, the chain operates above the oil level and a rotating disk picks up oil from the sump and deposits it onto the chain by means of a trough or collector plate.

OIL STREAM LUBRICATION—The lubricant is usually supplied by a pump that sprays oil onto the chain through nozzles. The stream should be directed to the lower, inside strand of chain. Excess will run off and return to pump. Oil should be changed periodically.

Properly lubricated chains will not show brownish color at the joints and the connecting link pins will be brightly polished.

REPAIRING CHAIN DRIVES

1. To separate a roller chain, drive out the two pins of the link with alternate strokes, taking care not to damage adjacent links. If the pins have a head, grind them off before trying to remove. A chain-breaking tool is a quick, efficient method of removing links.

2. Sprocket life may be prolonged by reversing the sprockets, if the design permits. Be careful to check alignment.

3. Never insert a new link in a chain that has been elongated by wear. The new link will have a shorter pitch, causing shock when engaging the sprocket. This will soon destroy the chain.

4. Do not install a new chain on badly worn sprockets (Fig. 25). More damage will occur to the chain in a few hours than under years of normal use.

CLEANING OF CHAINS

Periodic cleaning is good economy under even the best operating conditions. Steps for chain cleaning are:

 Litho in U.S.A.

1. *Remove chain from sprockets.*
2. *Wash chain in diesel fuel.*
3. *Drain fuel and soak chain in oil.*
4. *Hang chain to drain off excess lubricant.*

STORING OF CHAINS AND SPROCKETS

Remove chain from sprockets, clean them, and coat with heavy grease. Then wrap chain in heavy grease-resistant paper and store in a dry area.

Sprockets may be left on shaft and coated with heavy protective grease.

Before using the drive again, thoroughly clean grease from the chains and sprockets, and re-lubricate the chain.

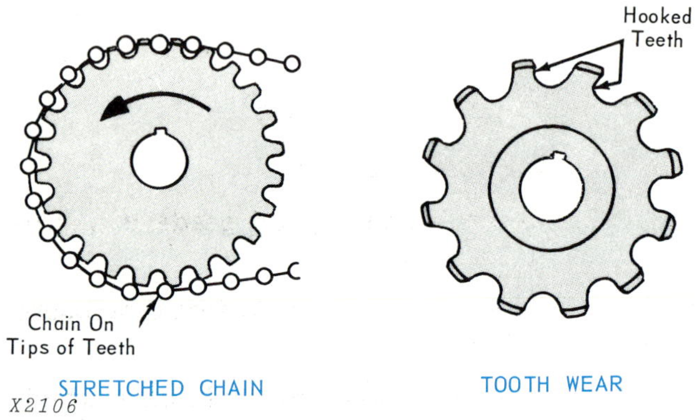

Fig. 25—Problems With Chain Drives

TROUBLE SHOOTING OF CHAIN DRIVES

Trouble	*Possible Cause*
Excessive noise	1. Misalignment of sprockets 2. Wrong tension 3. Lack of lubrication 4. Loose casings or bearings 5. Chain or sprocket worn out 6. Chain pitch too large
Wear on side bars, link plates, and sides of sprocket teeth	1. Misalignment
Chain climbing sprockets	1. Wrong chain or poor chain 2. Chain worn out 3. Lack of chain wrap on sprocket 4. Too much chain slack 5. Material build-up in sprocket tooth pockets 6. Worn sprockets
Broken pins, bushings, or rollers	1. Chain runs too fast 2. Heavy slack or sudden loads 3. Material build-up in sprocket tooth pockets 4. Lack of lubrication 5. Chain or sprocket corrosion 6. Wrong chain or worn sprockets
Chain clings to sprocket	1. Wrong chain or worn sprockets 2. Heavy or tacky lubricant 3. Excessive chain slack 4. Material build-up in sprocket tooth pockets
Chain whips	1. Too much slack in chain 2. High, pulsating loads 3. Stiff chain joints 4. Uneven wear on chain
Chain gets stiff	1. Lack of lubrication, resulting in wear 2. Corrosion 3. Excessive overloads 4. Material build-up in chain joint 5. Peening of side plate edges 6. Misalignment

Broken sprocket teeth	1. Obstruction or foreign material
	2. Excessive shock loads
	3. Chain climbing sprocket teeth
Chain fasteners fail	1. Vibration
	2. Obstructions striking fasteners
	3. Fasteners improperly installed
Drive runs too hot	1. Chain running too fast
	2. Lack of lubrication
	3. Chain immersed too deep in oil bath
	4. Chain or shafts rubbing against obstruction

GEAR DRIVES

Gears are the most common way to transmit power for heavier loads. With gears in mesh, all slippage is gone. Even the linkage of the chain is eliminated, giving more power potential.

OPERATION

Chapter 1 of this manual covers the basic gear types and their uses. Refer to that chapter for the basics of gear drive operation.

MAINTENANCE

The problems of *gear wear* and *backlash* are also explained in Chapter 1.

LUBRICATION

Gear lubricants range from simple mineral oils to complex formulas containing many ingredients.

For the type of oil to use, consult the manufacturer's operator's manual.

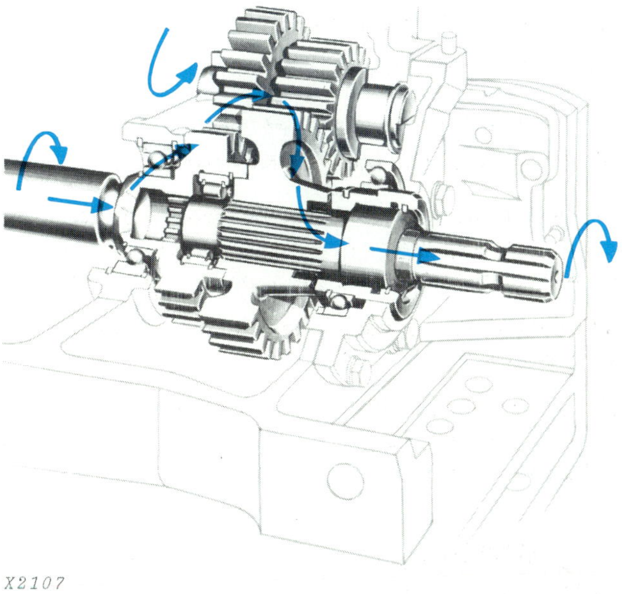

Fig. 26—Gear Drive

Common gear lubricants are:

SPUR GEARS—may use a good grade of petroleum oil—but not always.

BEVEL GEARS—may use an extreme-pressure (E.P.) lubricant.

WORM GEARS—may use an SCL lubricant, which offers even greater lubricant qualities.

Methods Of Lubricating Gears

Enclosed gearing is usually lubricated by the gears moving through a sump of oil and may have additional run-off troughs to lubricate the upper gears. The lubricant should be changed per the manufacturer's recommendations.

Open gears can be lubricated by:

1) Splash pan which the gears run through.

2) Hand lubrication by brushing or squirting (Fig. 27).

3) Automatic lubrication by a drip oiler.

Litho in U.S.A.

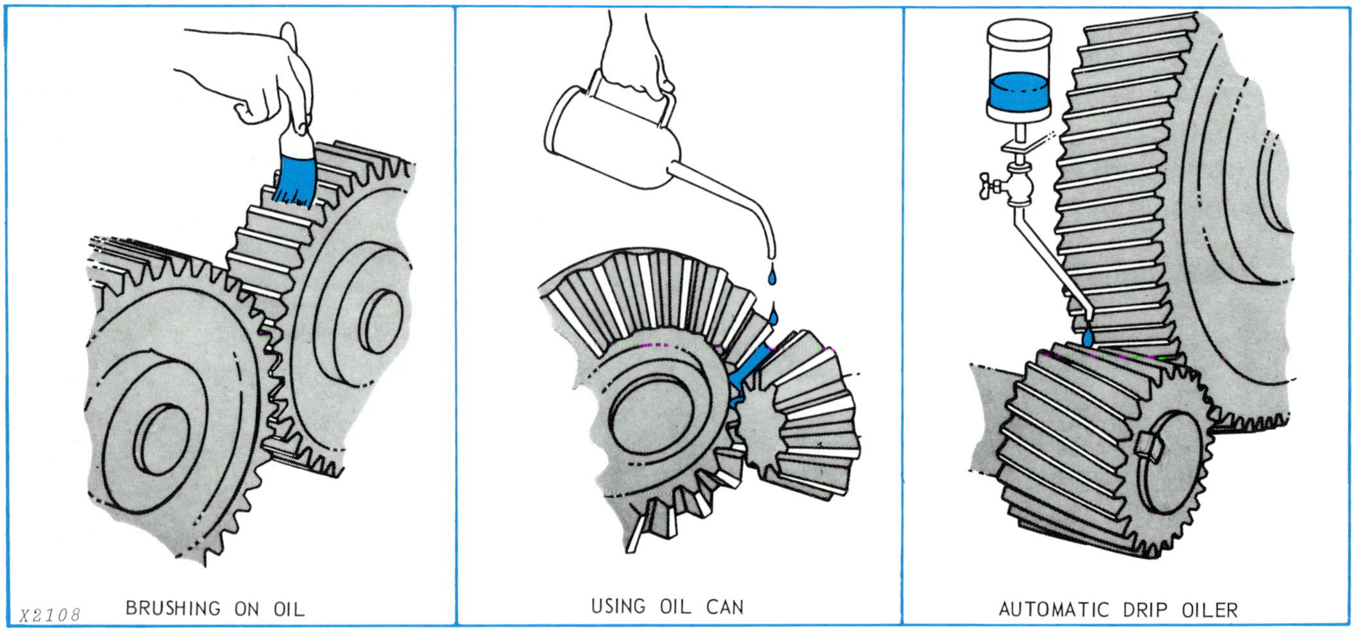

Fig. 27—Lubricating Of Open Gears—Three Ways

TROUBLE SHOOTING OF GEAR DRIVES

Trouble	*Possible Cause*
Fins around edge of teeth	1. Too much backlash
	2. Heavy, continuous loading
	3. Intermittent overloading
	4. Gears not hardened
Gear teeth appear burned from overheating	1. Too little backlash
	2. Overspeeding
	3. Overloading
	4. Lack of lubrication
Gear teeth are scored	1. Lack of proper lubrication
	2. Excessive speeds
	3. Overloading
	4. Too little backlash
Abrasions or fine tooth scratches	1. Dirt, grit, or metal particles in gears
Interference marks on tooth edges	1. Improper manufacturing
	2. Faulty assembly
Pitting of gear teeth	1. Excessive loading
Gouging near bottom of teeth	1. Too little backlash
Teeth broken	1. Too much backlash
	2. Shock impact or overload

RECIPROCATING DRIVES

Reciprocating drives change a *rotary* motion to a *linear* motion. The source of rotary motion could be the drives already discussed (belt, chain, gear) or the hydraulic or electrical devices.

A reciprocating mechanism is not actually a drive but is a supplement or helper for the drive.

Two uses of reciprocating drives: mowing cutter bars and plungerheads on hay balers.

Reciprocating drives are of four basic types:

- **Crankwheel and lever**
- **Crankarm and lever**
- **Off-center crankarm**
- **Cam**

Let's look at each one.

CRANKWHEEL AND LEVER DRIVE

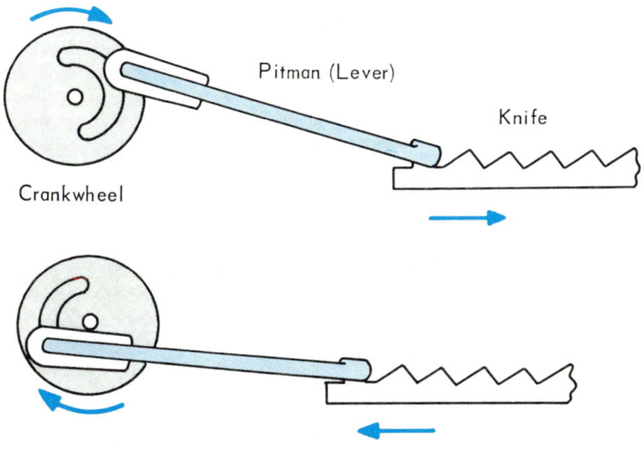

X2109

Fig. 28—Crankwheel and Pitman Lever Driving Mower Blade

The crankwheel and lever principle works from rotary motion (the crankwheel) with the lever or pitman attached off-center (Fig. 28). As the crankwheel turns, the pitman moves forward and back. One revolution of the crankwheel gives two strokes on the pitman. The mowing cutter bar uses this principle as shown.

Variations On Crankwheel And Lever Principle

A crankwheel and lever, with a *sway bar drive,* helps eliminate the up-and-down motion of the drive and reduces slapping and vibration (Fig. 29). As the pitman moves to the left (A), the knife is driven to the right. As the pitman moves to the right (B), the knife is driven to the left.

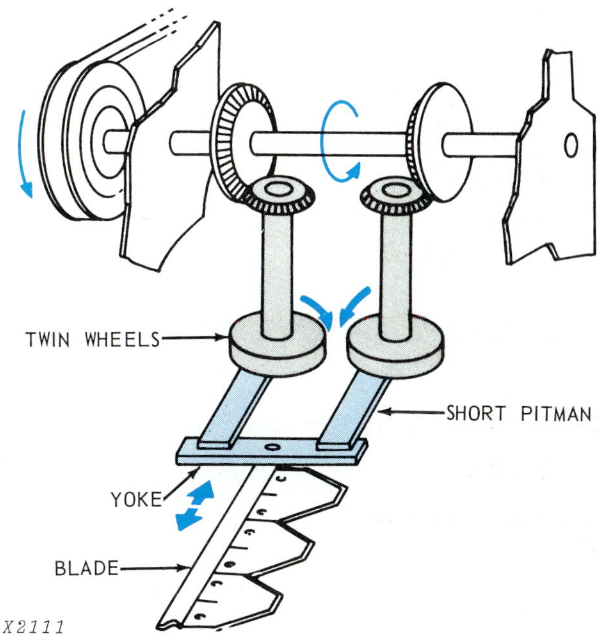

X2111

Fig. 30—Twin Wheel Drive Operating Mowing Cutter Bar

The *twin wheel drive* helps reduce vibration by having two crankwheels and short pitmans which operate in opposition to each other (Fig. 30).

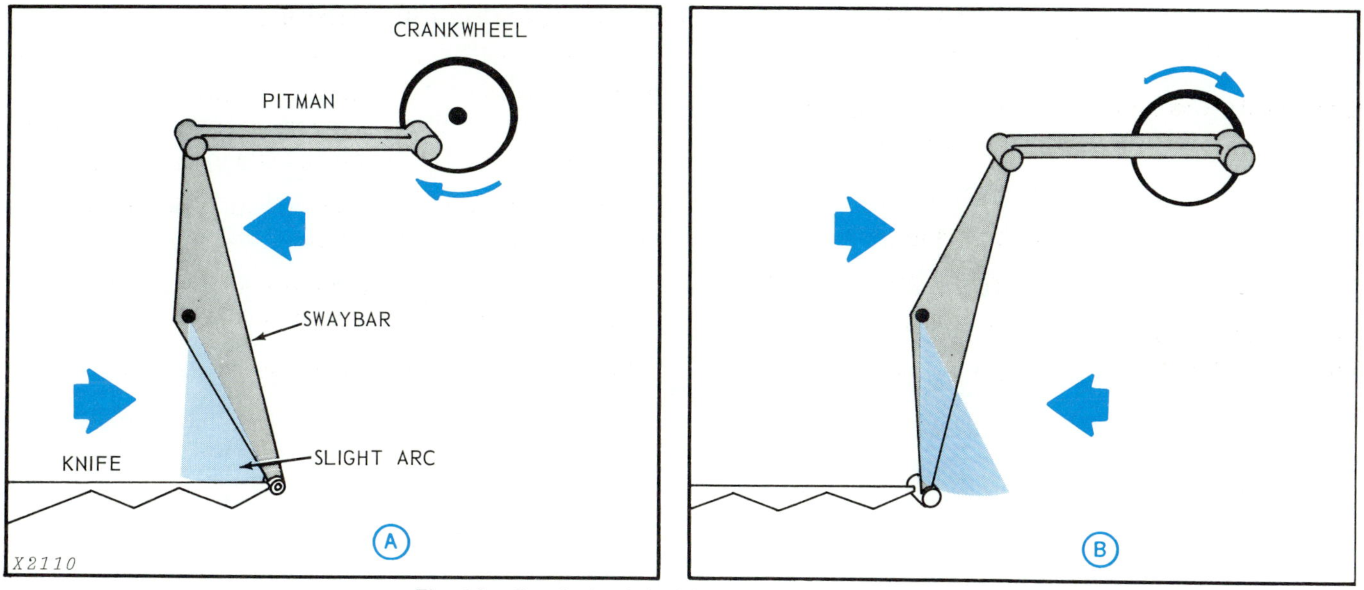

Fig. 29—Crankwheel And Lever With Swaybar Drive

CRANKARM AND LEVER DRIVE

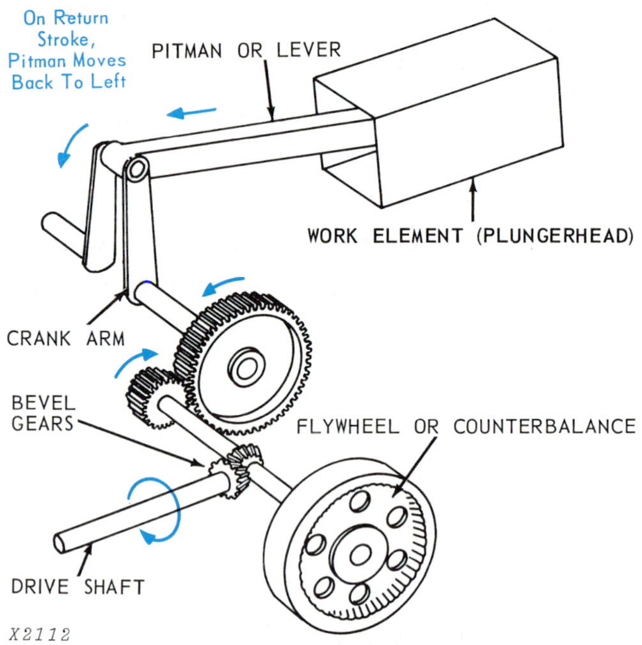

Fig. 31—Crankarm And Lever Drive For Hay Baler Plungerhead

A crankarm and lever drive is similar to a crankwheel and lever drive, except the crankarm takes the place of the crankwheel (Fig. 31).

Most reciprocating drives are counterbalanced to offset the inertia of the sudden changes in direction. This may be a counterweight, a dual drive, or a flywheel. The direction of the counterbalance is always the opposite of the pitman or lever.

OFF-CENTER CRANKARM DRIVE

The off-center crankarm drive is often called the *wobble shaft* or bent shaft drive (Fig. 32). As the shaft turns, the vertical motion is absorbed by a hinged yoke, while the horizontal motion is used for the back-and-forth motion.

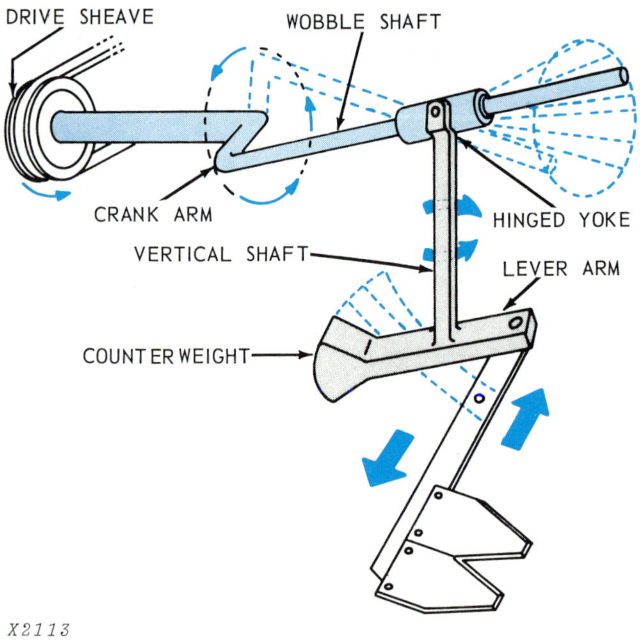

Fig. 32—Off-Center Crankarm Drive (Wobble Shaft) For Mower Cutterbar

A counterbalance is often used; however, the device can be used without a counterbalance if the weight of the machine is much greater than the force that must be driven. For example: It can be used as a sickle drive on a hay windrower because the sickle weight is very small in relation to the platform weight. But a counterweight must be used on a basic field mower because its weight is mainly in the cutter bar and drive.

CAM DRIVES

Cam drives are often used in a direct reciprocating motion (Fig. 33). Their action may also involve complicated or delayed motions. However, they always return to a starting point or reciprocate. Cam drives may use a spring load, gravity, or a track to return them to their starting positions as shown in Fig. 33.

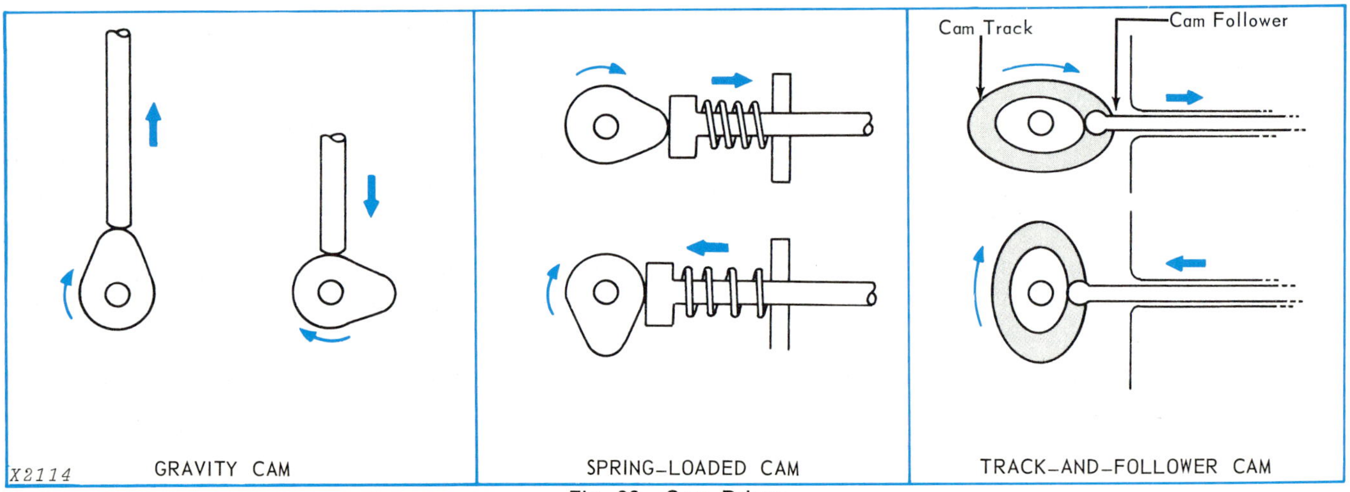

Fig. 33—Cam Drives

MAINTENANCE OF RECIPROCATING DRIVES

Lubrication is the key to good operation of all mechanical drives. Any moving part or parts making contact with another part should be well lubricated.

1) Bearings should be kept lubricated and checked for wear or damage periodically.

2) Cam tracks or cam surfaces require greasing for smooth operation and minimum wear.

3) Hinged areas need lubrication.

4) Enclosed drives should have oil level checked periodically.

5) Above all, refer to the machine operator's manual for proper lubrication.

TROUBLE SHOOTING OF RECIPROCATING DRIVES

Trouble usually starts in some place other than the reciprocating drive itself. Safety devices are usually built into the drive in some way to protect it. For this reason, belts are often used to drive reciprocating devices because the belt will slip and protect the drive in case of an obstruction. For the same reason, a wooden pitman stick which will break is often used on a mower.

Dirt contamination can be the cause of faulty operation of cams and crank drives and can lead to excessive wear. For this reason:

- **Clean drives periodically**
- **Keep shields in place**

Drive *alignment* is a must for proper reciprocation. Coordination is also needed between the power source, reciprocating drive, and work element.

This may mean:

1) Adjusting pitman length or length of stroke.

2) Adjusting cam track or follower.

3) Aligning lever and work element.

OVERLOAD RELEASE MECHANISMS FOR POWER TRAINS

In many modern machines one power source supplies many work functions. Each function has a different power requirement for its own work load.

Although it might take only 15 percent of total power to perform a certain function on a machine, more power is available, so a torque limiting factor or overload release mechanism is placed in the powerline to prevent damage in case an obstruction enters the machine.

Overload release mechanisms perform two functions:

1) Relieve shock on the power source.

2) Protect the machine part doing the work.

Overload mechanisms are of three major types:

- **Slip Clutches**
- **Jump Clutches**
- **Shear Pins**

Let's look at each one.

SLIP CLUTCHES

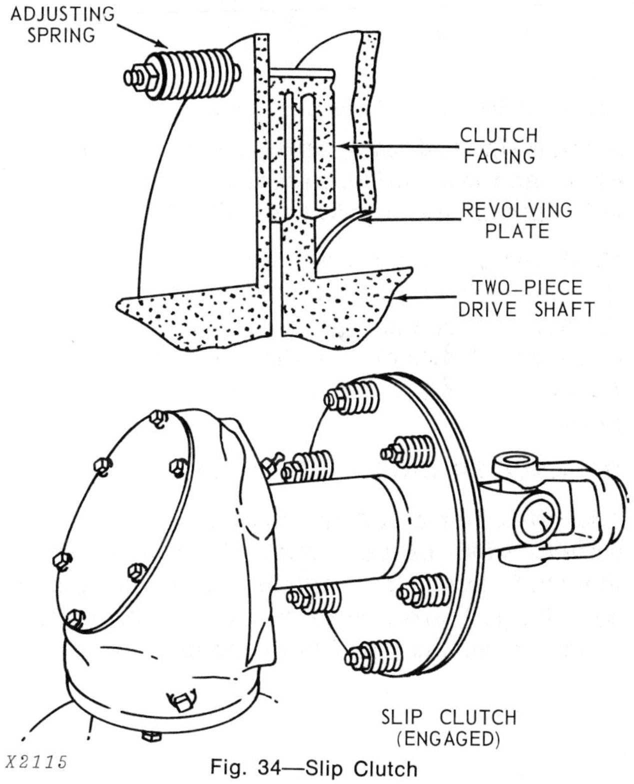

Fig. 34—Slip Clutch

Slip clutches work by friction (Fig. 34). The drive line is separated at the slip clutch, but linked together by means of clutch facings and spring tension.

During an obstruction, the friction force is overcome and the clutch slips, preventing damage to the machine and power line.

Tension can be either adjustable or non-adjustable and is supplied by springs or spring washers.

JUMP CLUTCHES

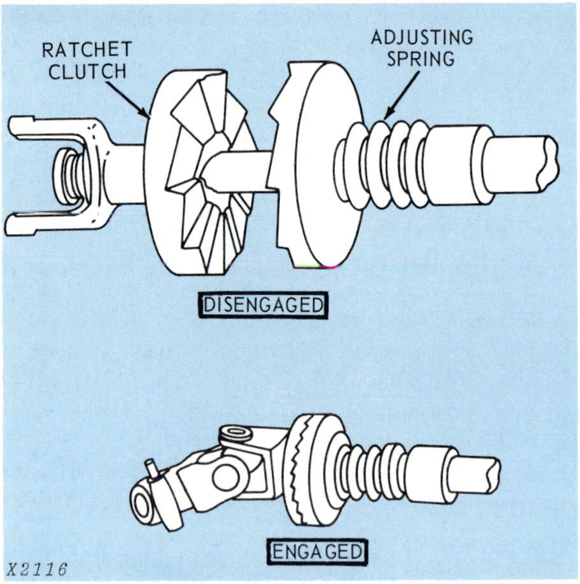

Fig. 35—Jump Clutch

The jump clutch (Fig. 35) does the same job as the slip clutch, although it is not as widely used. The power line connection is joined by a two-piece ratchet. One piece supplies the power, while the other receives and transmits power to the power line. The ratchet is held together by spring tension, which is adjustable.

In case of overload, the spring tension is overcome and the ratchet slips, disengaging the power train to protect it.

SHEAR PINS

Shear pins (Fig. 36) work on the stress principle. A pin or bolt will break if too much force is exerted on it. Size and hardness of pin varies according to the stress needs of the power train.

Again, the power train is actually two pieces, with a shear pin connecting them. In case of overload, the pin shears and disconnects the powerline.

Shear pins are simple and relatively inexpensive, and so are widely used. The major disadvantage is that each time a pin is sheared the operation is stopped and the pin must be replaced.

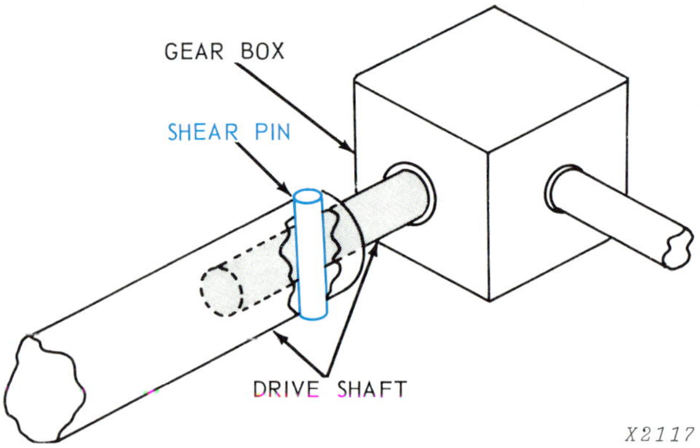

Fig. 36—Shear Pin In Power Driveline

MAINTENANCE OF OVERLOAD MECHANISMS

Lubrication

Lubrication is generally simple in an overload mechanism. Remember these points:

1) A light coating of oil can be used to keep clutch faces from sticking.

2) Too much oil on clutch faces reduces friction and causes slipping.

3) Spring tension for safety mechanisms may require light lubrication.

4) Shafts that are actually separated, but run inside a connecting shaft, should be lubricated to inhibit rust and corrosion that may prevent disengagement of the powerline.

General Maintenance

Specifications for overload *release* mechanism adjustment and setting should be closely followed and can be found in the machine operator's manual.

Many slip clutches and jump clutches are adjusted.

Be sure to replace shear pins with the exact duplicates. Refer to the machine parts catalog. Many times a shear pin is in the form of a bolt, and the bolt strength and size should be closely checked before installation.

TROUBLE SHOOTING OF OVERLOAD MECHANISMS

Trouble	*Possible Cause*
Slip clutch continually slips	1. Too little spring tension, Belleville washer worn out 2. Oiled or glazed clutch facings 3. Improper assembly 4. Failure of the working element 5. Internal shaft frozen to external shaft
Slip clutch will not slip	1. Facings have become stuck 2. Too much spring tension 3. Improper assembly
Jump clutch continually jumps	1. Too little spring tension 2. Ratchet worn out 3. Ratchet surface is slick from lubricant 4. Dirt build-up not permitting complete contact between ratchet teeth 5. Working element not functioning 6. Drive overloaded
Jump clutch will not jump	1. Too much spring tension 2. Spring bottomed out 3. Ratchet frozen due to rust or corrosion 4. Dirt preventing operation of spring release or ratchet
Shear pin continually shears	1. Wrong shear pin or bolt 2. Working element not functioning 3. Drive overloaded
Shear pin will not shear	1. Wrong shear pin or bolt 2. Internal shaft frozen to external shaft

TEST YOURSELF

QUESTIONS

1. What are the three major kinds of special drives?

2. Which one is a friction drive?

3. How do the pulleys change belt speed in a variable speed drive?

4. True or false? "If one belt breaks in a multiple set, you need not replace all the belts."

5. Should the idler be on the tight or slack side of the chain?

6. Reciprocating drives change a ________ motion into a ________ motion.

(Answers on page 10 in back of text.)

DEFINITIONS OF TERMS AND SYMBOLS

A

ABRASION—Wearing or rubbing away of a part.

ALIGNMENT—An adjustment to a line or to bring into a line.

ANTI-CLOCKWISE ROTATION—Rotating the opposite direction of the hands on a clock. The same as counter-clockwise rotation.

ANTI-FRICTION BEARING—A bearing constructed with balls, rollers or the like between the journal and the bearing surface to provide rolling instead of sliding friction.

ASAE—American Society of Agricultural Engineers.

ASME—American Society of Mechanical Engineers.

AXIAL—Parallel to the shaft or bearing bore.

AXLE—The shaft or shafts of a machine upon which the wheels are mounted.

AUTOMATIC TRANSMISSION—A transmission in which gear or ratio changes are self-activated.

B

BACKLASH—The clearance or "play" between two parts, such as meshed gears.

BALL BEARING—An anti-friction bearing consisting of a hardened inner and outer race with hardened steel balls which roll between the two races.

BDC—Bottom dead center.

BEARING—The supporting part which reduces friction between a stationary and rotating part.

BEVEL SPUR GEAR—Gear that has teeth with a straight center-line cut on a cone.

BONDED LINING—A method of cementing brake linings to shoes or bands which eliminates the necessity of rivets.

BRAZE—To join two pieces of metal with the use of a comparatively high melting point material. An example is to join two pieces of steel by using brass or bronze as a solder.

BREAK-IN—The process of wearing-in to a desirable fit between the surfaces of two new or reconditioned parts.

BROACH—To finish the surface of metal by pushing or pulling a multiple-edge cutting tool over or through it.

BURNISH—To smooth or polish by the use of a sliding tool under pressure.

BUSHING—A removable liner for a bearing.

C

CARRIER—An object that bears, cradles, moves, or transports some other object or objects.

CASE-HARDEN—To harden the surface of steel.

CASTELLATE—Formed to resemble a castle battlement, as in a castellated nut.

CENTER OF GRAVITY—The point at which a mass of matter balances. For example, the center of gravity of a wheel is the center of the wheel hub.

CENTRIFUGAL FORCE—A force which tends to move a body away from its center of rotation. Example: whirling a weight attached to a string.

CHAMFER—A bevel or taper at the edge of a hole or a gear tooth.

CHASE—To straighten up or repair damaged threads.

CHILLED IRON—Cast iron on which the surface has been hardened.

CLEARANCE—The space allowed between two parts, such as between a journal and a bearing.

CLUTCH—A device for connecting and disconnecting the engine from the transmission or for a similar purpose in other units.

COEFFICIENT OF FRICTION—The ratio of the force resisting motion between two surfaces in contact to the force holding the two surfaces in contact.

COMPOUND—A mixture of two or more ingredients.

CONCENTRIC—Two or more circles, having a common center.

 Litho in U.S.A.

CONSTANT MESH TRANSMISSION—A transmission in which the gears are engaged at all times, and shifts are made by sliding collars, clutches or other means to connect the gears to the output shaft.

CONTRACTION—A reduction in mass or dimension; the opposite of expansion.

CORRODE—To eat away gradually as if by gnawing, especially by chemical action.

COUNTERBORE—To enlarge a hole to a given depth.

COUNTER-CLOCKWISE ROTATION—Rotating the opposite direction of the hands on a clock.

COUNTERSHAFT—An intermediate shaft which receives motion from a main shaft and transmits it to a working part. Sometimes called a lay shaft.

COUNTERSINK—To cut or form a depression to allow the head of a screw to go below the surface.

COUPLING—A connecting means for transferring movement from one part to another; may be mechanical, hydraulic, or electrical.

D

DEAD AXLE—An axle that only supports the machine and does not transmit power.

DEFLECTION—Bending or movement away from normal due to loading.

DENSITY—Compactness; relative mass of matter in a given volume.

DIAGNOSIS—A systematic study of a machine or machine parts to determine the cause of improper performance or failure.

DIAL INDICATOR—A measuring instrument with the readings indicated on a dial rather than on a thimble as on a micrometer.

DIFFERENTIAL GEAR—The gear system which permits one drive wheel to turn faster than the other.

DIRECT DRIVE—Direct engagement between the engine and driveshaft where the engine crankshaft and the driveshaft turn at the same rpm.

DISTORTION—A warpage or change in form from the original shape.

DOUBLE REDUCTION AXLE—A drive axle construction in which two sets of reduction gears are used for extreme reduction of the gear ratio.

DOWEL PIN—A pin inserted in matching holes in two parts to maintain those parts in fixed relation one to another.

DRIVE LINE—The universal joints, drive shaft and other parts connecting the transmission with the driving axles.

DROP FORGING—A piece of steel shaped between dies while hot.

DUAL REDUCTION AXLE—A drive axle construction with two sets of pinions and gears, either of which can be used.

E

ECCENTRIC—One circle within another circle wherein both circles do not have the same center. An example of this is a cam on a camshaft.

ENDPLAY—The amount of axial or end-to-end movement in a shaft due to clearance in the bearings.

F

FEELER GAUGE—A metal strip or blade finished accurately with regard to thickness used for measuring the clearance between two parts; such gauges ordinarily come in a set of different blades graduated in thickness by increments of 0.001 inch.

FILLET—A rounded filling between two parts joined at an angle.

FIT—The contact between two machined surfaces.

FLANGE—A projecting rim or collar on an object for keeping it in place.

FLUID DRIVE—A drive in which there is no mechanical connection between the input and output shafts, and power is transmitted by moving oil. (See Chapter 6 on Torque Converters.)

FOOT POUND (or lbs. ft.)—This is a measure of the amount of energy or work required to lift 1 pound a distance of 1 foot.

FREE-WHEELING CLUTCH—A mechanical device which will engage the driving member to impart motion to a driven member in one direction but not the other. Also known as an "overrunning clutch."

 Litho in U.S.A.

G

GEAR—A cylinder- or cone-shaped part having teeth on one surface which mate with and engage the teeth of another part which is not concentric with it.

GEAR RATIO—The ratio of the number of teeth on the larger gear to the number of teeth on the smaller gear.

GRIND—To finish or polish a surface by means of an abrasive wheel.

H

HEAT TREATMENT—Heating, followed by fast cooling, to harden metal.

HEEL—The outside, larger half of the gear tooth.

HELICAL—Shapes like a coil spring or a screw thread.

HELICAL GEAR—Gears with the teeth cut at an angle to the axis of the gear.

HERRINGBONE GEAR—A pair of helical gears designed to operate together. The angle of the pair of gears forms a V.

HUB—The central part of a wheel or gear.

HYDRAULIC PRESSURE—Pressure exerted through the medium of a liquid.

HYPOID GEAR—A gear that is similar in appearance to spiral bevel gear, but the teeth are cut so that the gears match in a position where the shaft centerlines do not meet.

I

ID—Inside Diameter.

IMPELLER—The pump or driving member in a torque converter.

INPUT SHAFT—The shaft carrying the driving gear by which the power is applied, as to the transmission.

J

JOURNAL—A bearing with a hole in it for a shaft.

K

KEY—A small block inserted between the shaft and hub to prevent circumferential movement.

KEYWAY—A groove or slot cut to permit the insertion of a key.

KNURL—To indent or roughen a finished surface.

L

LAPPING—The process of fitting one surface to another by rubbing them together with an abrasive material between the two surfaces.

LINKAGE—Any series of rods, yokes, and levers, etc., used to transmit motion from one unit to another.

LIVE AXLE—A shaft that transmits power from the differential to the wheels.

LOST MOTION—Motion between a driving part and a driven part which does not move the driven part. Also see Backlash.

LOW SPEED—The gearing which produces the highest torque and lowest speed of the wheels.

M

MISALIGNMENT—When bearings are not on the same centerline.

MULTIPLE DISK—A clutch with a number of driving and driven disks as compared to a single plate clutch.

N

NEEDLE BEARING—An anti-friction bearing using a great number of long, small-diameter rollers. Also known as a quill bearing.

O

OD—Outside diameter.

OSCILLATE—To swing back and forth like a pendulum.

OUTPUT SHAFT—The shaft or gear which delivers the power from a device, such as a transmission.

OVERDRIVE—Any arrangement of gearing which produces more revolutions of the driven shaft than of the driving shaft.

OVERRUN COUPLING—A free-wheeling device to permit rotation in one direction but not in the other.

P

PEEN—To stretch or clinch over by pounding with the rounded end of a hammer.

PINION—The smaller of two meshing gears.

PINION CARRIER—The mounting or bracket which retains the bearings supporting a pinion shaft.

PLANETARY GEAR SET—A system of gearing which is modeled after the solar system. A pinion is surrounded by an internal ring gear and planet gears are in mesh between the ring gear and pinion around which all revolves.

PLANET CARRIER—In a planetary gear system, the carrier or bracket in a planetary system which contains the shafts upon which the pinions or planet gears turn.

PLANET GEARS—The gears in a planetary gear set which connect the sun gear to the ring gear.

POWER SHIFT TRANSMISSION—A transmission in which gear changes are selected manually but are power actuated; no master clutch is involved.

PRELOAD—A load within the bearing, either purposely built in, or resulting from adjustment.

PRESS FIT—Mounting with interference, i.e., bore of bearing is smaller than OD of shaft, or OD of bearing is larger than bore of housing, or both.

PUMP—A device which produces motion in a liquid. In a torque converter, the driving member. (Also see "Impeller")

R

RACE—A channel in the inner or outer ring of an anti-friction bearing in which the balls or rollers roll.

RADIAL—Perpendicular to the shaft or bearing bore.

RADIAL CLEARANCE (Radial displacement)—Clearance within the bearing and between balls and races perpendicular to the shaft.

RADIAL LOAD—A force perpendicular to the axis of rotation.

RATIO—The relation or proportion that one number bears to another.

REACTOR—See "Stator"

REAM—To finish a hole accurately with a rotating fluted tool.

RECIPROCATING—A back-and-forth movement, such as the action of a piston in a cylinder.

RING GEAR—A gear which surrounds or rings the sun and planet gears in a planetary system. Also the name given to the spiral bevel gear in a differential.

RIVET—A headed pin used for uniting two or more pieces by passing the shank through a hole in each piece, and securing it by forming a head on the opposite end.

ROLLER BEARING—An inner and outer race upon which hardened steel rollers operate.

RPM—Revolutions per minute.

S

SAE—Society of Automotive Engineers.

SCORE—A scratch, ridge or groove marring a finished surface.

SEAT—A surface, usually machined, upon which another part rests or seats; for example, the surface upon which a valve face rests.

SEPARATORS—A component in an anti-friction bearing which keeps the rolling components apart.

SHIM—Thin sheets used as spacers between two parts, such as the two halves of a journal bearing.

SHRINK-FIT—Where the shaft or part is slightly larger than the hole in which it is to be inserted. The outer part is heated above its normal operating temperature or the inner part chilled below its normal operating temperature or both and assembled in this condition; upon cooling an exceptionally tight fit is obtained.

SLIDING-FIT—Where sufficient clearance has been allowed between the shaft and journal to allow free-running without overheating.

SLIDING GEAR TRANSMISSION—A transmission in which gears are moved on their shafts to change gear ratios.

SLIP-IN BEARING—A liner made to extremely accurate measurements which can be used for replacement purposes without additional fitting.

FOS—40 (Jun—69) Litho in U.S.A.

SPIRAL BEVEL GEAR--A ring gear and pinion wherein the mating teeth are curved and placed at an angle with the pinion shaft.

SPIRAL GEAR—A gear with teeth cut according to a mathematical curve on a cone. Spiral bevel gears that are not parallel have center lines that intersect.

SPLINE—Splines are multiple keys in the general form of internal and external gear teeth, used to prevent relative rotation of cylindrically-fitted parts.

SPUR GEAR—Gears cut on a cylinder and the teeth are straight and parallel to the axis.

SQ. FT.—Square feet

SQ. IN.—Square inch

STALL CONDITION—A condition in a torque converter when the driving element (pump) is turning and the driven element (turbine) is stopped. Stall produces maximum vortex flow (see Chapter 6 on Torque Converters).

STATOR—In a torque converter, the third member (in addition to turbine and pump) which changes direction fluid under certain operating conditions.

STRESS—The force to which a material, mechanism, or component is subjected.

SUN GEAR—The central gear in a planetary gear system around which the rest of the gears rotate.

SYNCHROMESH TRANSMISSION—Transmission gearing which aids the meshing of two gears or shift collars by matching their speed before engaging them.

SYNCHRONIZE—To cause two events to occur at the same time. For example, to bring two gears to the same speed before they are meshed.

T

TAP—To cut threads in a hole with a tapered, fluted, threaded tool.

TEMPER—To change the physical characteristics of a metal by applying heat.

TENSION—Effort which elongates or "stretches" a material.

THRUST LOAD—A load which pushes or reacts through the bearing in a directon parallel to the shaft.

TOLERANCE—A permissible variation between the two extremes of a specification or dimension.

TORQUE—A twisting motion, usually measured in ft-lbs (N-M).

TORQUE CONVERTER—A turbine device utilizing a rotary pump, one or more reactors (stators) and a driven circular turbine or vane whereby power is transmitted from a driving to a driven member by hydraulic action. It provides varying drive ratios; with a speed reduction, it increases torque.

TORQUE WRENCH—A special wrench with a built-in indicator to measure the applied force.

TORUS SECTION—The confines of a flow circuit in a radial plane in a torque converter or fluid coupler.

TRANSAXLE—Type of construction in which the transmission and differential are combined in one unit.

TRANSMISSION—An assembly of gears, or other elements which gives variations in speed or direction between the input and output shafts.

TROUBLESHOOTING—A process of diagnosing the source of the trouble or troubles through observation and testing.

TUNE-UP—A process of accurate and careful adjustments to obtain the best performance.

TURBINE—A rotary device for obtaining mechanical power from a pressurized flow of gases or liquids.

TURBULENCE—A disturbed or irregular motion of fluids or gases.

V

VANES—Any plate, blade or the like attached to an axis and moved by air or a liquid.

VORTEX—A whirling movement or mass of liquid or air.

W

WORM GEAR—A gear with teeth that resemble a thread on a bolt. It is meshed with a gear that has teeth similar to a helical tooth except that it is dished to allow more contact.

 Litho in U.S.A.

INDEX

P **Page**

R

S

S (Cont.) **Page**

T

U

V

W

ANSWERS TO TEST YOURSELF QUESTIONS

ANSWERS TO CHAPTER 1 QUESTIONS

1. a — 2; b — 3; c — 1.

2. Gear B has traveled ½ revolution.

3. False. To reduce speeds, a small gear drives a larger one.

4. Reducing gear speeds will **increase** the twisting force or torque.

5. True.

6. Friction, gear, fluids.

7. **Friction** — wheels, belts, clutches, etc. **Gears** — transmissions, chains, etc. **Fluids** — water wheel, torque converter, fluid drive, etc.

8. Any one of these: Operate more quietly, wear less rapidly, have greater tooth strength.

9. 1. Reduce friction; 2. Support a shaft.

10. Preloaded.

11. Endplay.

12. Backlash.

ANSWERS TO CHAPTER 2 QUESTIONS

1. Any four of these: Disk, plate, band, overrunning, cone, expanding shoe.

2. Wet and dry.

3. Any two of these: Long wearing, heat resistant, allow little slippage.

4. The flexible disk has springs around its hub.

5. First blank **engage.** Second blank **free wheel.**

6. False — Overcenter linkage locks both while engaged and disengaged.

7. False.

8. **Both** grabbing and slipping (No. 3).

ANSWERS TO CHAPTER 3 QUESTIONS

1. Sliding gear, collar shift, and synchromesh.

2. True.

3. The collar shift transmission usually runs quieter than a sliding gear type. (This is because it can use helical — instead of spur-tooth gears.)

4. Synchromesh.

5. The countershaft serves to transmit and vary the power flow between the input and output shafts.

6. Helical.

7. A chamfer is a rounded area or bevel or the edge of gear teeth, etc. (It helps to make gears mesh easier when they are shifted.)

ANSWERS TO CHAPTER 4 QUESTIONS

1. First blanks — hydraulic clutches. Second blanks — gear train.

2. Countershaft and planetary.

3. **Underdrive** means that the output shaft turns **slower** than the input, while **overdrive** means that the output turns **faster** than the input.

4. Sun gear, planet pinions (and carrier), and ring gear.

5. True.

6. The ratio is 1 to 1 (a direct drive).

7. 1) Lubricates (and cools), 2) engages the clutches and brakes.

ANSWERS TO CHAPTER 5 QUESTIONS

1. First blank — low. Second blank — high.

2. Torque converter uses fluids at **high** speeds but relatively **low** pressures.

3. **Pump** and **motor**.

4. Variable.

5. The charge pump **makes** up for oil lost from the closed circuit between the pump and motor.

ANSWERS TO CHAPTER 6 QUESTIONS

1. First two blanks — fluid coupling. Second two blanks — torque converter.

2. The stator.

3. First blank — vortex. Second blank — rotary.

4. False.

5. False.

6. a — 3; b — 1; c — 2.

Litho in U.S.A.

ANSWERS TO CHAPTER 7 QUESTIONS

1. Transmits power "around the corner" and allows each wheel to rotate at a different speed.

2. They lock out differential action to prevent a loss of power when one wheel slips.

3. Mechanical, hydraulic, automatic.

4. To prevent the danger of turning the machine with the differential lock engaged.

5. The automatic (no-spin) type.

6. False. The faster wheel turns faster than ring gear speeds, but the slower wheel turns the same as the ring gear.

ANSWERS TO CHAPTER 8 QUESTIONS

1. Straight axle, pinion, planetary, chain.

2. Straight axle.

3. A *live* axle transmits the torque as well as supporting part of the machine's weight. The *dead* axle only supports the machine.

4. False.

5. Either of these answers: More compact; more durable.

6. The main advantage: Allows for high clearance under the axle. The main disadvantage: Tends to loosen at the chain.

ANSWERS TO CHAPTER 9 QUESTIONS

1. a — 2; b — 3; c — 1.

2. They have a different number of splines (540 has six splines, while 1000 has twenty-one splines).

3. True.

ANSWERS TO CHAPTER 10 QUESTIONS

1. Belt, chain, gear.

2. Belt.

3. The two halves of the pulley move closer together or farther apart to move the belt in or out.

4. False.

5. On the slack side.

6. First blank — rotary. Second blank — linear or straight.

Litho in U.S.A.

Miss Conserves

Mes secrets et mes 85 meilleures recettes

PRATICO EDITION

SOMMAIRE

Le bonheur est dans les pots

Quand j'ai mis, bien maladroitement, mes premiers poivrons en pots en 2005, j'étais loin de me douter où ça me mènerait 15 ans plus tard !

Bien que les membres de ma famille aient toujours été des passionnés de cuisine, aimant se rassembler autour d'une bonne table et s'impliquant dans des cuisines, des restos et des boucheries, personne ne fait de conserves dans mon entourage.

C'est donc par curiosité que je me suis lancée, avec un peu d'innocence, dans la fabrication de conserves maison. J'ai été étonnée, comme plusieurs je crois, de trouver autant d'informations contradictoires en ligne. Elles se divisaient entre les règles de sécurité et les « on a toujours fait comme ça et on n'a jamais été malades ». J'ai donc poursuivi mes lectures et mes essais, qui étaient parfois réussis, parfois désastreux !

À force de faire plus de conserves et de voir la réaction si positive des gens de mon entourage quand je leur offrais un peu de bonheur en pots, j'ai réalisé que ce nouvel univers devenait une véritable passion. Puisque l'entrepreneuriat m'avait toujours intéressée, j'ai décidé de partir ma petite affaire et de vendre mes propres conserves un peu partout !

J'ai suivi avec beaucoup d'enthousiasme une formation sur la mise en conserve commerciale. Malheureusement, c'est avec beaucoup de déception que j'ai réalisé que mes maigres économies ne suffiraient pas à répondre à toutes les attentes en matière de salubrité, d'assurances et d'investissements nécessaires à la création de ma propre conserverie. Toutefois, ma passion pour les conserves n'était pas morte, et j'échangeais toujours sur le sujet avec un groupe de gens merveilleux sur Facebook. Après ma formation, j'ai réalisé que j'étais en mesure d'aider les gens, de les conseiller et de leur offrir des trucs pour réussir leurs propres conserves.

C'est ainsi qu'en janvier 2016, j'ai organisé mon premier atelier, chez moi, à Sorel. Je savais que, comme ç'a été le cas pour moi au départ, l'autoclave effrayait plusieurs personnes qui souhaitaient faire des conserves. Et c'est de là que tout est parti : j'ai donné des ateliers de mise en conserve de Bonaventure à Val-D'Or, en passant par Québec. Des gens de partout dans la province partageaient ma passion et avaient besoin d'un p'tit coup de main pour se lancer dans cet art d'une autre époque.

On m'a déjà dit que j'avais un passe-temps de grand-mère, pour une fille de mon âge... Mais il n'y a pas d'âge pour vouloir mettre du bonheur en pots, pas plus qu'il n'y a d'âge pour apprendre ! C'est donc avec le plus grand plaisir que je donne mes ateliers à des gens de tous les horizons : de jeunes mamans, des grands-parents, des chasseurs, des étudiants, etc. Et c'est grâce à toute cette belle aventure que je vous présente aujourd'hui un recueil des délicieuses recettes accumulées au fil du temps et des belles rencontres qui m'ont inspirée.

Sab

L'abc des **conserves réussies**

Une fois, j'ai dit : « Si je devais énumérer tous les avantages de la mise en conserves maison, il faudrait que j'écrive un livre tellement il y en a ! » Alors, puisque j'écris justement un livre, en voici quelques-uns.

Les conserves permettent de gagner du temps. Quel bonheur d'avoir des pots, des repas prêts-à-manger qu'il suffit de réchauffer, sans devoir penser à les décongeler la veille, sans avoir à acheter un congélateur supplémentaire et à craindre les pannes d'électricité !

Ça permet aussi d'économiser ! Oui, bien sûr, au début il y a des dépenses à faire : un autoclave, des pots, des instruments de cuisine... Mais ces articles sont réutilisés chaque année. Puis, quand on cuisine de grosses quantités, on magasine les rabais, on profite des bas prix des produits de saison et on fait des achats en groupe pour économiser.

On découvre nos agriculteurs locaux, on encourage les circuits courts, on découvre aussi des nouveaux produits, fruits et légumes, des nouvelles saveurs.

On mange mieux, moins de repas au resto ou de plats pour emporter de l'épicerie. On contrôle mieux le contenu de notre assiette (ou de nos pots !) en n'y mettant que du bon, des aliments qui répondent aux contraintes alimentaires de notre famille, en fonction de la santé de tous les membres.

C'est sans oublier les bienfaits pour l'environnement ! Réutiliser des pots en verre plutôt que d'opter pour des produits présentant des emballages jetables, prioriser les aliments locaux plutôt que ceux qui ont parcouru la moitié de la planète, éviter le gaspillage alimentaire en rescapant des fruits et des légumes moins beaux : à quoi bon la tomate parfaite si c'est pour en faire du coulis ?

Et dire que tout cela est possible grâce à des pots en verre ! Bien que la mise en conserve soit un art qui se pratique depuis plus de 150 ans, gardons toujours en tête que c'est un exploit que d'arriver à conserver des aliments à température ambiante pendant plusieurs mois, et que cela demande le respect de règles bien précises.

Tous ces bons arguments peuvent entraîner un excès de bonne volonté et d'enthousiasme. Je le sais bien : je suis passée par là moi aussi à mes débuts. Allez-y en douceur pour commencer, un pot à la fois, une recette à la fois. C'est bien stimulant de revenir du marché les bras pleins de beaux produits frais à l'air délicieux, mais il est tout aussi décourageant d'éteindre la cuisinière à 2 h du matin et de n'avoir fait que le quart de tout ce qu'on s'était imaginé. Allez-y à votre rythme : prenez le temps de bien maîtriser votre autoclave et votre cuisinière, posez des questions et planifiez !

Planifier, planifier, réviser, contre-vérifier et... planifier !

Je me prépare toujours au moins un jour à l'avance avant d'empoter quoi que ce soit. Je lis la recette au complet plusieurs fois. Je fais un inventaire de tous les ingrédients et dresse une liste des choses à acheter. Je prépare tout le matériel nécessaire, bien sûr les pots et l'équipement de mise en conserves, mais aussi les casseroles, les planches à découper, les bols, les couteaux, etc.

N'oubliez pas que pour un temps donné de stérilisation, il faudra attendre que la chaleur monte ; c'est du temps à ajouter à votre planification, en plus du nettoyage après. Mais ne vous découragez pas : les premières expériences seront peut-être difficiles (d'où l'importance de voir petit pour commencer), mais vous en apprendrez beaucoup sur la gestion du temps. Au fil des pots, on en arrive à s'organiser pour canner 18 bocaux de rôti un mardi soir d'hiver en réchauffant un truc canné pour souper.

Les conditions favorables au développement de la bactérie *Clostridium botulinum*

Voici trois aspects à prendre en considération pour limiter la prolifération de cette bactérie responsable du botulisme et assurer la salubrité d'une conserve.

- **Absence d'oxygène.** L'absence d'oxygène est propice au développement de la bactérie *Clostridium botulinum*. En plus des conserves, pensons notamment aux emballages sous vide ou aux préparations recouvertes d'une couche d'huile.
- **Humidité.** Il faut un minimum d'eau pour que la bactérie se multiplie.
- **Aliments peu acides.** La volaille et les viandes, poissons, légumes et fines herbes fraîches sont des exemples d'aliments peu acides, et donc plus sujets au développement de la bactérie. Les aliments acides tels que certains fruits, le jus de citron ou le vinaigre, quant à eux, peuvent empêcher sa prolifération.

La mise en conserve: une question d'acidité

Le premier pas avant de sélectionner la méthode de mise en conserve appropriée? Connaître le degré d'acidité (pH) des aliments. On le détermine grâce à un pH-mètre, soit l'instrument utilisé pour mesurer le pH (potentiel hydrogène). Retenez qu'un pH de 4,6 correspond à la limite critique, celle où la *Clostridium botulinum* est susceptible de se développer. En deçà de cette valeur, un aliment est considéré comme étant suffisamment acide pour limiter le développement de la toxine et il peut donc être stérilisé à la casserole. En revanche, un aliment dont le pH est supérieur à 4,6 est peu acide et, donc, il doit être stérilisé à l'autoclave. Cette marmite atteint une température supérieure (116 °C – 240 °F) à celle de la stérilisation à la casserole (100 °C – 212 °F).

Lorsqu'on stérilise des conserves à la casserole, leur pH doit atteindre 4,2, et ce, même si la limite critique est fixée à 4,6: cela permet de se laisser une marge de manœuvre et d'assurer une stérilisation sécuritaire. Toutes les recettes faites à la casserole présentées dans ce livre respectent cette norme et ont été testées.

On acidifie avec...

Du jus de citron en bouteille

Le jus de citron en bouteille permet d'uniformiser le taux d'acidité. Évitez le jus de citron frais, car son taux d'acidité varie d'un fruit à l'autre.

De l'acide citrique

Les mots «acide citrique» peuvent paraître intimidants à priori. C'est pourtant une substance qui est naturellement présente dans certains fruits, dont les agrumes. On la produit de nos jours à grande échelle et on l'utilise dans une multitude de domaines. Elle est largement utilisée par l'industrie alimentaire pour ses propriétés acidifiantes et de conservation, notamment dans les conserves, les jus et les boissons, les pâtes à pain, les produits laitiers, etc. On peut s'en procurer dans certaines pharmacies, épiceries, magasins d'aliments naturels ou autres commerces en ligne. **Il ne faut pas omettre ou substituer cet ingrédient** dans les recettes qui en contiennent, à moins de pouvoir mesurer de façon adéquate le pH final de la recette avec un pH-mètre.

Du vinaigre

Les vinaigres ne sont pas tous égaux en matière d'acidité et de goût. Il importe de choisir un vinaigre dont le taux d'acide acétique est indiqué sur l'emballage. Les recettes de ce livre ont été testées avec des vinaigres à 5% d'acide acétique. Les vinaigres à 7% d'acide acétique sont sécuritaires, mais beaucoup plus forts et acides au goût. On peut, par exemple, remplacer un vinaigre blanc à 5% par un vinaigre de vin toujours à 5%, qui sera plus doux et plus sucré au goût.

Le mot d'ordre: VIGILANCE

La mise en conserves est une opération simple, mais qui nécessite une vigilance accrue afin de limiter les risques d'intoxication alimentaire et d'empêcher la prolifération de la *Clostridium botulinum*. Cette bactérie très résistante peut produire la toxine botulique, une substance dangereuse pour l'humain. En effet, elle peut nuire à la transmission du signal nerveux entre les nerfs et les muscles, et ainsi provoquer la paralysie, voire un décès. En vous assurant de respecter les mesures d'hygiène, les étapes de stérilisation, la température requise, les temps de traitement ainsi que les proportions des recettes à la lettre, vous aurez l'esprit tranquille. Portez également une attention particulière aux conditions d'entreposage recommandées.

Attention aux livres de recettes de conserves plus vieux: même si les recettes y sont intéressantes, les directives de mise en conserves ne sont plus nécessairement à jour.

Mise en conserve: les méthodes

Le choix de la méthode de stérilisation dépendra du taux d'acidité des recettes. S'il s'agit de **recettes acides (pH inférieur à 4,2)**, on réalisera la stérilisation à l'aide d'une casserole d'eau bouillante. Les confitures, gelées, chutneys, ketchups, aliments marinés dans le vinaigre, fruits et tomates additionnées de jus de citron sont quelques exemples d'aliments associés à cette technique. Les **recettes peu acides (pH égal ou supérieur à 4,2)** doivent être stérilisées à l'autoclave afin d'éliminer les risques de botulisme. L'autoclave est une casserole haute comportant un couvercle à verrou et un régulateur de pression conçu pour une mise en conserve sécuritaire sous pression à très haute température. Les mets à base de viande, de poisson ou de légumes, par exemple, requièrent cette méthode.

Validation du pH

Le pH de chacune des recettes de ce livre a été minutieusement mesuré et testé à l'aide d'un pH-mètre bien calibré. Inutile, donc, de vous procurer votre propre pH-mètre pour le mesurer.

Ne modifiez pas une recette à bas pH sans avoir les compétences et l'équipement nécessaires pour vous assurer de la sécurité de la recette. Les bandelettes de mesure de pH ne sont pas assez précises pour les besoins de la mise en conserve.

Ne consommez jamais un aliment peu acide qui a été stérilisé à la casserole d'eau bouillante alors qu'il aurait dû l'être à l'autoclave.

Les techniques à éviter

Assurez-vous de différencier l'autoclave de marque Presto et le «presto» (autocuiseur): les autocuiseurs, bien qu'ils fonctionnent de la même façon qu'un autoclave, ne permettent pas de connaître la pression exacte qu'ils génèrent. La connaissance de cette pression est essentielle pour atteindre une température suffisamment élevée pour détruire les bactéries dangereuses. Contrairement à certaines pratiques courantes, la préparation de conserves au four, au micro-ondes ou au lave-vaisselle est à proscrire, car les risques d'intoxication à la bactérie *Clostridium botulinum* sont élevés. En effet, ces techniques ne sont pas adaptées à cette pratique et ne peuvent garantir une mise en conserve sécuritaire, et ce, même si vous ou l'un de vos proches avez déjà réussi une mise en conserve en utilisant l'une d'entre elles.

Mes conseils pour réussir vos conserves

S'il y a une méthode de conservation qui exige de la précision et de la minutie, c'est bien la mise en conserves! Voici trois éléments à respecter à la lettre.

1. **L'espace de tête.** Laissez toujours un espace entre le couvercle et le contenu du pot. La raison est bien simple: au cours de la stérilisation, les aliments prennent de l'expansion et exercent une pression permettant d'expulser l'air hors du bocal. Or, si le pot est trop rempli (ou pas assez), l'étanchéité du couvercle risque d'être compromise. L'espace de tête à respecter dépend du type d'aliment et du mode de stérilisation. Il est mentionné pour chaque recette.

2. **La recette.** Cela peut sembler évident, mais le respect des ingrédients, de la température, du temps (de cuisson et de stérilisation) et du niveau de pression recommandé est essentiel pour empêcher la bactérie *Clostridium botulinum* de se développer. En effet, chaque recette a été élaborée en tenant compte de ces facteurs ainsi que du taux d'acidité des aliments.
3. **La quantité et la taille des aliments en fonction de la taille des pots.** Les temps de stérilisation tiennent compte de la densité des aliments, qui influence la vitesse à laquelle la chaleur les pénètre. Pour cette raison, il est impératif de respecter la taille des dés, des cubes ou des juliennes.

Matériel requis

- **Bocaux.** Les pots de type « Mason » sont vendus sous les marques Bernardin, Golden Harvest, Ball et Kerr. Évitez les pots à charnière et les pots récupérés du commerce (exemple : vieux pot de mayonnaise, de salsa ou de cornichon). Assurez-vous que les pots sont en bon état et que le verre est intact et non ébréché. Ils doivent être dotés d'un goulot fileté conçu pour les bagues de mise en conserves.
- **Disques et bagues (couvercles).** Le disque est le couvercle plat en acier étamé doté d'un produit d'étanchéité, tandis que la bague est l'élément métallique que l'on ajuste sur le goulot afin de maintenir le disque en place.
- **Cuillère trouée.** Il vous faudra une cuillère trouée ou un autre ustensile troué pour empoter les solides avant les liquides. Évitez le bois, car il a tendance à absorber le goût des aliments. Les ustensiles en acier inoxydable sont à privilégier.
- **Louche.** Cet instrument sert simplement à transvider les préparations liquides dans les bocaux lors de l'empotage.
- **Entonnoir.** Rien de mieux pour vous permettre de transférer les aliments dans vos pots sans en mettre partout !
- **Pinces pour bocaux.** Utilisez toujours les pinces pour manipuler les pots pleins et chauds, surtout pour les déplacer à l'intérieur et en dehors de la casserole et de l'autoclave. Elles sont conçues à cet effet, avec un bout en caoutchouc antidérapant qui permet une prise ferme sur le verre des pots, pour éviter de vous brûler.
- **Balance et tasses à mesurer.** Mesurez ou pesez vos aliments avec précision. Une balance de cuisine est particulièrement utile pour les grosses quantités. Des tasses et des cuillères à mesurer propres sont essentielles pour respecter les proportions.
- **Minuterie.** Utilisez une minuterie avec alarme sonore pour vous assurer de bien respecter tous les temps à calculer.
- **Chiffon ou essuie-tout propre et vinaigre blanc.** Il est essentiel d'utiliser un chiffon propre ou un essuie-tout imbibé de vinaigre blanc pour nettoyer les impuretés sur le rebord des bocaux après les avoir remplis.

Pas besoin de mesurer l'espace de tête, car les pots eux-mêmes indiquent les mesures : le filet le plus haut se situe à 0,5 cm (¼ de po) du couvercle et celui du bas à 1 cm (½ po), tandis que l'anneau se trouve à 2,5 cm (1 po).

Bulles d'air : pourquoi les éliminer ?

Après avoir brassé la préparation, son volume pourrait diminuer et ainsi modifier l'espace de tête, empêchant potentiellement le disque de bien sceller le pot. C'est pourquoi il est essentiel de remuer la préparation afin de retirer les bulles d'air, et ce, avant de mesurer l'espace de tête.

Les étapes de stérilisation

Voyez les étapes de stérilisation et d'empotage. Pour les étapes de stérilisation des pots remplis à la casserole, rendez-vous à la page 19. Pour celles dédiées à la stérilisation à l'autoclave, référez-vous aux consignes de la page 20.

Avant de commencer

Vos bocaux doivent toujours être propres et intacts. **Notez que depuis 2008, les fabricants ont démontré qu'il est inutile de stériliser les couvercles et les bocaux avant l'utilisation :** la stérilisation à la casserole ou à l'autoclave des pots remplis suffit à détruire toutes les bactéries présentes, tant que les bocaux sont propres au moment de l'utilisation. De plus, contrairement à ce que l'on a longtemps cru, l'écart de température n'est pas suffisant pour causer un choc thermique. On peut laver les pots et les instruments de mise en conserves au lave-vaisselle pendant que l'on prépare la recette.

Précisions sur l'empotage

- Une fois les aliments cuisinés, versez la préparation dans les pots à l'aide d'une cuillère trouée ou d'une louche et d'un entonnoir. La préparation doit être très chaude, voire bouillante, à moins d'indication contraire.
- Éliminez les bulles d'air en remuant la préparation. Pour ce faire, glissez délicatement un ustensile le long du bocal, c'est-à-dire entre la paroi et la préparation. Assurez-vous également que l'espace de tête correspond aux indications de la recette. Rectifiez la quantité au besoin.
- Les impuretés peuvent nuire au scellage hermétique : nettoyez bien le rebord des bocaux à l'aide d'un chiffon propre ou d'un essuie-tout imbibé de vinaigre blanc.
- Déposez les disques sur les bocaux. Vissez la bague à une main : lorsque vous parvenez au point de résistance (lorsque le pot tourne sur lui-même), vissez environ 2,5 cm (1 po) supplémentaires. Les bagues vissées trop serrées vont déformer les disques, mais si elles ne le sont pas suffisamment, elles ne se scelleront pas sur l'ouverture du pot.

La stérilisation des pots une fois ceux-ci remplis

Pour les recettes au pH inférieur à 4,2 : à la casserole

Conseils pour choisir sa casserole

Presque n'importe quelle casserole pourra convenir pour la stérilisation à l'eau bouillante. Optez pour une casserole au fond épais et de grand format : sa profondeur devrait être supérieure de 7,5 cm (3 po) à la hauteur des bocaux. Les pots ne doivent pas être en contact direct avec le fond de la casserole. Pour surélever les pots, on peut placer des bagues au fond de la casserole, partie plate (dessus) vers le haut.

Sachez qu'un autoclave est aussi une grande casserole qui vient avec une grille au fond. Si vous ne verrouillez pas le couvercle et que vous ne mettez pas la pesée, votre autoclave pourra servir pour les deux techniques de stérilisation !

Tenir compte de l'altitude

La durée du traitement des aliments stérilisés à la casserole varie en fonction de l'altitude : lorsqu'on canne au niveau de la mer, les temps de stérilisation indiqués dans les recettes sont les bons. **Par contre, si on canne au-delà de 300 mètres (1000 pi) d'altitude, il faut ajouter 5 minutes aux temps indiqués dans les recettes stérilisées à la casserole seulement.** Au Québec, 90 % du territoire habité se situe sous les 300 mètres. Pour connaître le niveau d'élévation de la zone où vous vous trouvez, demandez à Google, téléchargez une application ou informez-vous auprès de votre municipalité. N'oubliez pas de vous informer de l'altitude si vous vous déplacez, par exemple au chalet ou chez des amis.

Étapes de stérilisation à la casserole

ÉTAPE 1

Versez de l'eau et 30 ml (2 c. à soupe) de vinaigre blanc dans la casserole et portez l'eau à ébullition. **Attention : en ajoutant les pots, le niveau d'eau va monter.** Utilisez des pinces pour déposer les bocaux sur le support dans la casserole, en prenant soin de les recouvrir d'eau (au moins 2,5 cm – 1 po d'eau au-dessus des couvercles). Portez de nouveau à ébullition, puis commencez à calculer la durée de la stérilisation recommandée dans la recette à partir de ce moment.

ÉTAPE 2

Une fois le traitement terminé, éteignez le feu et retirez les bocaux avec la pince prévue à cet effet, en prenant soin de garder les bocaux droits, puis déposez-les sur une grille ou une planche de bois. Laissez-les refroidir 12 heures sans les manipuler.

Pour les recettes au pH égal ou supérieur à 4,2: à l'autoclave

Se procurer un bon autoclave

L'autoclave est une casserole conçue pour la mise en conserves sécuritaire des aliments à faible taux d'acidité: elle permet de détruire les spores responsables du développement du botulisme grâce à son couvercle verrouillable ainsi qu'à un régulateur de pression (pesée), permettant d'atteindre une température élevée (116 °C – 240 °F). Bien des modèles sont proposés selon votre budget (entre 80 $ et 350 $). Notez que deux grandes marques sont offertes dans les magasins à grande surface, dans les boutiques spécialisées ou chez Miss Conserves: All American ainsi que T-Fal (autrefois Mirro). Parmi ces marques, on trouve deux types de fonctionnements.

À manomètre. Ce cadran à aiguille greffé à l'autoclave permet de mesurer la pression à l'intérieur de l'autoclave: il faut demeurer près de l'appareil pendant toute la durée du traitement afin de surveiller l'aiguille et de voir à ce que la pression demeure stable. Les manomètres sont des instruments de mesure qui se décalibrent avec le temps. Vous devez donc faire calibrer votre manomètre chaque année pour vous assurer qu'il indique la bonne pression. **Pour cette raison, le fabricant Presto a retiré les manomètres de ses autoclaves pour les remplacer par une pesée plus précise qui ne se décalibre jamais.** Les autoclaves à manomètre viennent aussi avec une ou plusieurs pesées, qu'il est nécessaire de mettre en place pour créer la pression dans l'autoclave.

À pesée (régulateur de pression). Ce type de fonctionnement permet de maintenir la pression à 5, 10 ou 15 psi (*pound per square inch*). Il n'est pas nécessaire de constamment garder l'autoclave à l'œil pendant toute la durée du traitement: on peut se fier au mouvement ou au sifflement de la pesée (on l'entend bien). Certains modèles ont une seule pesée pourvue de trois positions, d'autres ont une seule pesée qui se défait en trois parties, et d'autres encore sont dotés de trois pesées distinctes de 5, 10 et 15 psi chacune.

Si vous avez un autoclave de marque Presto avec manomètre, vous pouvez écrire à la compagnie pour demander gratuitement une pesée 5-10-15 pour les modèles de moins de dix ans afin d'éviter de faire calibrer votre manomètre chaque année.

On peut empiler plusieurs bocaux dans l'autoclave (sauf les formats de 1 litre): il suffit de les placer de manière à ce qu'ils se chevauchent, ou de déposer une seconde grille plate et perforée entre les étages. Attention: les boutons de la grille ne doivent jamais être appuyés contre les disques des pots déposés dessous. Ma solution: enfoncer les boutons de la grille au moyen d'un marteau, ou encore, se procurer une tôle perforée résistante (par exemple, une plaque à pizza).

L'altitude: un facteur qui influence la pression

Vous cannez au niveau de la mer? Misez sur une pression de 10,5 psi. Au-delà de 300 mètres (1000 pi) d'altitude, on augmente la pression à 15 psi. Renseignez-vous pour connaître votre niveau d'altitude et assurez-vous de toujours respecter les recommandations du manuel d'instruction de votre autoclave en ce qui concerne l'altitude.

Étapes de stérilisation à l'autoclave

ÉTAPE 1

Préparez les aliments en suivant la recette. Juste avant d'empoter la nourriture, préparez votre autoclave. Ajoutez de l'eau dans la cuve selon les spécifications du fabricant (habituellement 3 litres) et 30 ml (2 c. à soupe) de vinaigre blanc, puis portez à ébullition. Déposez les pots sur la grille du fond à l'aide de pinces à bocaux. Il est à noter que le liquide ne devrait pas recouvrir les pots. On fait ici un traitement à la vapeur, non pas à l'eau bouillante.

LE SAVIEZ-VOUS?
En ajoutant de 30 à 250 ml (de 2 c. à soupe à 1 tasse) de vinaigre dans l'eau selon le taux de calcaire qu'elle renferme, vous éviterez que des dépôts de minéraux ne tachent vos bocaux ou l'intérieur de l'autoclave.

ÉTAPE 2

Verrouillez le couvercle. Faites chauffer l'autoclave à feu élevé, jusqu'à ce que l'évent se dresse (l'évent est le mécanisme qui verrouille le couvercle de l'autoclave sur la cuve). Calculez 10 minutes pour ventiler la cuve de l'autoclave. Cette étape est très importante, car elle permet de faire sortir les poches d'air à l'intérieur de l'autoclave et de ne conserver que la vapeur d'eau. Après les 10 minutes, déposez la pesée sur la soupape d'évacuation selon les indications du fabricant (déposée ou enclenchée).

Certains couvercles scellent en silence. Le fameux bruit de « pop » n'est pas un gage de réussite ou d'échec! Il faudra vérifier plus tard si les bocaux sont bien scellés.

Les autoclaves de marque All American possèdent un couvercle qui est maintenu en place sur la cuve à l'aide de grosses poignées vissées; ils ne sont donc pas dotés d'un évent. Il vous faut alors surveiller attentivement la soupape d'évacuation et calculer 10 minutes à partir du moment où vous voyez un puissant jet de vapeur constant en sortir.

ÉTAPE 3

Quand la pression parvient au bon niveau selon votre altitude (soit la pesée se mettra à bouger, soit le manomètre bien calibré vous l'indiquera), commencez à calculer la durée de traitement indiquée dans la recette, puis baissez graduellement et doucement la chaleur de la cuisinière pour maintenir cette pression aussi stable que possible tout au long de la durée de stérilisation. Si vous utilisez une pesée 5-10-15, celle-ci devrait bouger sans arrêt, mais doucement.

ÉTAPE 4

Une fois le traitement terminé, coupez la chaleur de votre cuisinière de moitié, puis attendez 5 minutes avant de l'éteindre complètement. Laissez l'autoclave refroidir de lui-même. Il ne faut jamais retirer l'autoclave du rond avant que la pression soit redescendue : il est très chaud et très pesant et pourrait vous blesser gravement. Ne bougez pas l'autoclave avant que la pression soit complètement redescendue, c'est-à-dire quand l'évent redescend ou quand le manomètre indique 0 psi et qu'aucune vapeur ne s'échappe de la soupape d'évacuation quand vous soulevez la pesée. Portez des mitaines de four pour ouvrir l'autoclave. Au moment de retirer les bocaux à l'aide des pinces, assurez-vous de garder ceux-ci bien droits. Déposez-les sur une grille ou une planche de bois. Une période de refroidissement de 12 heures est nécessaire avant de toucher ou d'entreposer les pots.

La première utilisation d'un autoclave peut être un événement stressant ou intimidant. Je vous recommande d'essayer d'abord avec un pot rempli seulement d'eau avant de vous lancer dans une recette. Je vous invite aussi à suivre un atelier avec moi pour voir et entendre toutes les étapes de A à Z afin de vous familiariser avec toutes celles de la mise en conserve!

Après le traitement à l’autoclave ou à la casserole

Après avoir laissé reposer vos conserves pendant 12 heures, assurez-vous que vos bocaux sont bien scellés : retirez les bagues et soulevez les pots par le disque. Si nécessaire, nettoyez les pots (passez un linge humide propre sur les couvercles, le filetage et la surface des bocaux). Étiquetez chaque conserve, puis entreposez-les dans un endroit frais et sombre (un garde-manger ou un placard, par exemple), en évitant les sources de chaleur. Si les couvercles ne sont pas scellés, réfrigérez les conserves immédiatement, et consommez leur contenu dans les jours qui suivent ou congelez-le. Ne remettez pas les bagues sur les pots.

CONSERVATION 101

Si vous avez respecté à la lettre les étapes de mise en conserve, et si vous entreposez vos conserves à l'abri de la lumière et de la chaleur, vous pouvez espérer conserver certaines conserves au meilleur de leur qualité jusqu'à douze mois.

Ensuite, il y aura une dégradation lente des couleurs, des saveurs et des textures. Cela ne signifie pas qu'on doit tout jeter après douze mois, mais il est préférable de consommer les conserves plus anciennes en premier et de tenir un inventaire à jour avant de planifier une nouvelle production.

Sachez qu'à partir de l'ouverture du bocal, la durée de conservation ne sera plus la même. Il faudra entreposer la conserve au réfrigérateur, et la durée de conservation sera la même que pour un produit similaire du commerce. Par exemple: plusieurs mois pour une marinade, cinq jours pour une recette avec de la viande.

Le sel

Le sel de table contient de l'iode et des agents anti-agglutinants. L'iode décolore les aliments sur une longue période de temps. Puisqu'on met des aliments en conserve pour les manger beaucoup plus tard, il est très fortement recommandé d'utiliser un sel sans additifs, comme du gros sel (également appelé «sel à marinade» ou «sel kasher»). Notez que le sel de mer, la fleur de sel ou le sel himalayen contiennent naturellement une petite quantité d'iode, et sont beaucoup plus dispendieux que le gros sel vendu en épicerie ou en vrac. Je recommande donc toujours du gros sel pour toutes les recettes de conserves.

Les quantités, multiplications et divisions

Justement pour des raisons de goût, bien que je souhaite que mes recettes plaisent à tous, je vous recommande de les essayer en petite quantité la première fois. Toutes les recettes (sauf celle qui contient de la pectine) peuvent être multipliées et divisées pour correspondre à la quantité spécifique que vous souhaitez canner. Soyez aussi précis que possible, utilisez une calculatrice au besoin et revérifiez vos calculs deux fois plutôt qu'une!

Les goûts et les modifications

«Les goûts ne se discutent pas!» dit le vieil adage. Le processus de stérilisation, surtout à l'autoclave, peut modifier l'intensité des saveurs, surtout des épices. Certaines personnes les trouvent amplifiées, d'autres les trouvent diminuées ou amoindries, et d'autres encore les trouvent inchangées. Je vous présente dans ce livre les recettes selon mes goûts. Je vous recommande malgré tout de goûter à vos préparations avant de les empoter et d'ajuster au besoin les épices et assaisonnements (sauf sur indications contraires dans la recette). Gardez en tête qu'il est plus simple d'ajouter des épices plus tard que d'en retirer. Allez-y donc plus doucement la première fois que vous faites une recette et ajustez la prochaine fois.

Vous aurez surement remarqué que j'aime la cuisine très épicée. Les piments me passionnent et j'en cultive plusieurs dizaines de variétés chez moi! Outre leur côté piquant, ils renferment une multitude de saveurs et de parfums différents. Je suis bien consciente que la chaleur des piments ne plaît pas aux palais et aux estomacs de tous. Vous pouvez, dans toutes les recettes, changer le type (la force) des piments utilisés, les remplacer par des flocons de piment, par une quantité équivalente en poids ou en volume de poivron doux ou les omettre complètement lorsque vous voyez la mention «facultatif».

Indices pour repérer une «mauvaise» conserve

Si, au moment de l'ouverture d'une conserve, celle-ci dégage une mauvaise odeur ou présente d'autres signes apparents de détérioration, ou si le couvercle n'offre aucune résistance ou ne fait pas de son («pop»), ne prenez pas de chance et évitez de consommer le contenu. Cependant, il est normal que la préparation change légèrement de couleur avec le temps (les aliments seront plus foncés et auront l'air plus ternes).

BASES

Les recettes de base sont celles que l'on aime tous avoir en réserve dans le garde-manger. Elles sont souvent l'élément principal d'un repas ou d'une autre recette de conserves. Ces recettes vous permettront de vous familiariser avec les techniques de base de la mise en conserves et de découvrir l'utilisation de votre autoclave comme autocuiseur. Découvrez des recettes de bouillons, des protéines nature à ajouter à d'autres plats et plusieurs mélanges d'épices et de fines herbes maison pour rehausser vos mets.

PAR PORTION 1 pot de 500 ml	
Calories	102
Protéines	5 g
M.G.	1 g
Glucides	22 g
Fibres	7 g
Fer	2 mg
Calcium	57 mg
Sodium	36 mg

Coulis de tomates

STÉRILISATION

QUANTITÉ TOTALE • 10 LITRES (40 TASSES)

Taille des pots	Temps de stérilisation
250 ml (4 oz)	30 minutes
500 ml (8 oz)	30 minutes
1 litre (16 oz)	30 minutes

À la casserole

Préparation
30 minutes

Cuisson
2 heures

- **sans œuf**
- **sans produits laitiers**
- **sans noix**
- **végé**
- **sans gluten**

11,36 kg (25 lb) de tomates italiennes bien mûres

300 ml (environ 1 ¼ tasse) de jus de citron en bouteille

1 pincée de sel et/ou de sucre (facultatif)

1. Laver les tomates, puis retirer les parties abîmées, le cas échéant.

2. Dans le contenant du robot culinaire, broyer les tomates jusqu'à ce que la peau et les pépins ne soient plus visibles.

3. Transvider les tomates broyées dans une grande casserole en acier inoxydable. Porter à ébullition, puis laisser mijoter de 2 à 3 heures à feu doux en remuant de temps à autre, jusqu'à ce que la préparation ait réduit de moitié, afin de laisser l'eau s'évaporer et de concentrer les saveurs.

4. Au fond de chaque pot, verser 15 ml (1 c. à soupe) de jus de citron pour les pots de 500 ml, et 30 ml (2 c. à soupe) de jus de citron pour les pots de 1 litre. Si désiré, ajouter une pincée de sel et/ou de sucre dans chaque pot.

5. Verser le coulis bouillant dans les bocaux, en laissant un espace libre de 1 cm (½ po) entre le coulis et le rebord des pots.

6. Plonger un ustensile dans les pots et le remuer afin d'éliminer toute bulle d'air. Au besoin, ajouter du coulis.

7. Stériliser à la casserole 30 minutes (pour des pots 250 ml, de 500 ml ou de 1 litre) selon les indications de la page 19.

!

Au Québec, les tomates italiennes sont de saison environ de la mi-août à la mi-octobre. Elles sont alors offertes à très bon prix, et leur saveur est à leur meilleur. Elles seront probablement cueillies avant leur maturité, alors prévoyez quelques jours pour les laisser mûrir à la noirceur, ou avisez votre maraîcher quelques jours avant votre visite pour avoir des tomates les plus savoureuses possible.

PAR PORTION 1 pot de 500 ml	
Calories	49
Protéines	2 g
M.G.	4 g
Glucides	0 g
Fibres	0 g
Fer	0 mg
Calcium	2 mg
Sodium	7 mg

Bouillon de bœuf

STÉRILISATION

QUANTITÉ TOTALE • 12 LITRES (48 TASSES)

Taille des pots	Temps de stérilisation
500 ml (16 oz)	35 minutes
1 litre (32 oz)	45 minutes

À l'autoclave

Préparation
25 minutes

Cuisson
1 heure
10 minutes

Temps de repos
4 heures

- **sans œuf**
- **sans produits laitiers**
- **sans noix**
- **sans gluten**

1 kg (environ 2 ¼ lb) de rôti de palette de bœuf avec os

1 kg (environ 2 ¼ lb) d'os de bœuf à bouillon cassés

2 gros oignons coupés en deux

4 grosses carottes entières avec les fanes

4 branches de céleri avec les feuilles

Sel au goût

3 feuilles de laurier

10 grains de poivre noir

15 ml (1 c. à soupe) de vinaigre de cidre

1. Préchauffer le four à 205 °C (400 °F).

2. Sur une plaque de cuisson antiadhésive, déposer le rôti de palette, les os de bœuf, les oignons, les carottes et le céleri. Cuire au four 40 minutes, en retournant le bœuf et les légumes à mi-cuisson.

3. Transvider le jus de cuisson dans l'autoclave, puis y déposer les ingrédients rôtis.

4. Déglacer la plaque avec un peu d'eau, en raclant le fond avec une cuillère en bois afin de détacher les sucs de cuisson, puis transvider le liquide dans l'autoclave.

5. Verser de l'eau jusqu'aux deux tiers de la cuve de l'autoclave. Saler. Ajouter les feuilles de laurier, le poivre et le vinaigre de cidre. Visser le couvercle de l'autoclave. Allumer le feu à élevé et placer la pesée de 15 psi sur la soupape d'évacuation (peu importe l'altitude). Il n'est pas nécessaire de laisser l'autoclave ventiler 10 minutes s'il sert pour la cuisson plutôt que pour la stérilisation.

6. À partir du moment où la pesée se met à bouger, cuire 30 minutes, en s'assurant de maintenir la pression à 15 psi.

7. Éteindre le feu et laisser la chaleur et la pression retomber d'elles-mêmes.

8. À l'aide d'une passoire fine, filtrer le bouillon contenu dans l'autoclave au-dessus d'un grand bol, puis le laisser reposer au frais 4 heures, jusqu'à ce que le gras fige à la surface (cela peut être dehors si la température est froide). Jeter les légumes et les os. Réserver le bœuf au frais pour une utilisation ultérieure.

9. Au moment de la mise en conserve, retirer le gras à la surface du bouillon à l'aide d'une cuillère.

10. Verser le bouillon dans une casserole en acier inoxydable et porter à ébullition. Goûter et rectifier l'assaisonnement au besoin. Si désiré, il est possible de faire réduire le bouillon davantage pour concentrer les saveurs.

11. Verser le bouillon bouillant dans les bocaux, en laissant un espace libre de 2,5 cm (1 po) entre le bouillon et le rebord des pots.

12. Stériliser à l'autoclave (35 minutes pour des pots de 500 ml et 45 minutes pour des pots de 1 litre) selon les indications de la page 20.

! Ici, on se sert de l'autoclave comme autocuiseur pour accélérer l'infusion du bouillon, puis on l'utilise de nouveau pour stériliser le bouillon dans les pots. Il est également possible de cuisiner le bouillon sur la cuisinière, puis de le stériliser à l'autoclave.

PAR PORTION 1 pot de 500 ml	
Calories	4
Protéines	0 g
M.G.	0 g
Glucides	1 g
Fibres	0 g
Fer	0 mg
Calcium	3 mg
Sodium	15 mg

Bouillon de légumes

STÉRILISATION

QUANTITÉ TOTALE • 12 LITRES (48 TASSES)

Taille des pots	Temps de stérilisation
500 ml (16 oz)	30 minutes
1 litre (32 oz)	35 minutes

À l'autoclave

Préparation
20 minutes

Cuisson
1 heure

- **sans œuf**
- **sans produits laitiers**
- **sans noix**
- **végé**
- **sans gluten**

2 gros oignons coupés en deux

3 grosses carottes entières avec les fanes

5 branches de céleri avec les feuilles

6 gousses d'ail (30 g)

15 ml (1 c. à soupe) d'huile végétale

Sel au goût

1 boîte de pâte de tomates de 156 ml

15 ml (1 c. à soupe) de miso

5 tiges de persil frais entières

5 branches de thym frais entières

2 feuilles de laurier

10 grains de poivre noir

1. Préchauffer le four à 205 °C (400 °F).

2. Dans un bol, déposer les oignons, les carottes, le céleri et l'ail. Ajouter l'huile et remuer. Saler.

3. Sur une plaque de cuisson antiadhésive, déposer la préparation aux légumes. Faire rôtir au four 30 minutes, en retournant les légumes à mi-cuisson.

4. Transvider le jus de cuisson dans l'autoclave, puis y déposer les ingrédients rôtis.

5. Déglacer la plaque avec un peu d'eau, en raclant le fond avec une cuillère en bois afin de détacher les sucs de cuisson, puis transvider le liquide dans l'autoclave.

6. Verser de l'eau jusqu'aux deux tiers de la cuve de l'autoclave. Saler. Ajouter la pâte de tomates, le miso, les fines herbes et le poivre. Visser le couvercle de l'autoclave. Allumer le feu à élevé et placer la pesée de 15 psi sur la soupape d'évacuation (peu importe l'altitude). Il n'est pas nécessaire de laisser l'autoclave ventiler 10 minutes s'il sert pour la cuisson plutôt que pour la stérilisation.

7. À partir du moment où la pesée se met à bouger, cuire 30 minutes, en s'assurant de maintenir la pression à 15 psi.

8. Éteindre le feu et laisser la chaleur et la pression retomber d'elles-mêmes.

9. À l'aide d'une passoire fine, filtrer le bouillon contenu dans l'autoclave au-dessus d'un grand bol. Goûter et rectifier l'assaisonnement au besoin. Si désiré, il est possible de faire réduire le bouillon davantage pour concentrer les saveurs.

10. Verser le bouillon bouillant dans les bocaux, en laissant un espace libre de 2,5 cm (1 po) entre le bouillon et le rebord des pots.

11. Stériliser à l'autoclave (30 minutes pour des pots de 500 ml et 35 minutes pour des pots de 1 litre) selon les indications de la page 20.

Bouillon
de légumes

Fumet de poisson et fruits de mer

PAR PORTION 1 pot de 500 ml	
Calories	37
Protéines	7 g
M.G.	1 g
Glucides	1 g
Fibres	0 g
Fer	1 mg
Calcium	42 mg
Sodium	167 mg

STÉRILISATION

QUANTITÉ TOTALE • 8 LITRES (32 TASSES)

Taille des pots	Temps de stérilisation
250 ml (8 oz)	40 minutes
500 ml (16 oz)	55 minutes
1 litre (32 oz)	70 minutes

À l'autoclave

Préparation
20 minutes

Cuisson
30 minutes

- **sans œuf**
- **sans produits laitiers**
- **sans noix**
- **sans gluten**

4 kg (8 ¾ lb) de carcasses (arêtes, têtes, queues, nageoires, etc.) de poisson, de homard, de crevettes ou de crabe

60 ml (¼ de tasse) de jus de citron

15 ml (1 c. à soupe) d'huile végétale

15 ml (1 c. à soupe) de miso

10 grains de poivre noir

6 gousses d'ail (30 g)

5 branches de céleri avec les feuilles

5 branches de thym frais entières

5 tiges de persil frais entières

3 grosses carottes entières avec les fanes

2 gros oignons coupés en deux

Sel au goût

1. Dans la cuve de l'autoclave, mélanger tous les ingrédients.

2. Verser de l'eau jusqu'aux deux tiers de la cuve de l'autoclave, puis visser le couvercle. Allumer le feu à élevé et placer la pesée de 15 psi sur la soupape d'évacuation (peu importe l'altitude). Il n'est pas nécessaire de laisser l'autoclave ventiler 10 minutes s'il sert pour la cuisson plutôt que pour la stérilisation.

3. À partir du moment où la pesée se met à bouger, cuire 30 minutes, en s'assurant de maintenir la pression à 15 psi.

4. Éteindre le feu et laisser la chaleur et la pression retomber d'elles-mêmes.

5. À l'aide d'une passoire fine, filtrer le fumet contenu dans l'autoclave au-dessus d'un grand bol. Goûter et rectifier l'assaisonnement au besoin. Si désiré, il est possible de faire réduire le fumet davantage pour concentrer les saveurs.

6. Répartir le fumet bouillant dans les bocaux, en laissant un espace libre de 2,5 cm (1 po) entre le fumet et le rebord des pots.

7. Stériliser à l'autoclave (40 minutes pour des pots de 250 ml, 55 minutes pour des pots de 500 ml et 70 minutes pour des pots de 1 litre) selon les indications de la page 20.

Les poissons et les fruits de mer ont des chairs délicates et à cuisson rapide. Ainsi, les stériliser longuement à l'autoclave ne leur rend habituellement pas hommage. Par contre, toutes leurs carcasses, retailles et coquilles vides peuvent être récupérées pour en faire un délicieux fumet à mettre en conserves, lequel pourra servir de base pour des soupes, des potages, des bisques et d'autres recettes, à condition d'ajuster le temps de stérilisation. Cela permet d'étendre l'utilité des produits de la mer – qui peuvent être coûteux! – ainsi que de réduire le gaspillage. Ne les jetez donc surtout pas! On peut accumuler les retailles et les carcasses de poisson et de fruits de mer dans un sac hermétique au congélateur jusqu'à ce que l'on en ait assez pour faire la recette.

PAR PORTION 1 pot de 500 ml	
Calories	416
Protéines	29 g
M.G.	1 g
Glucides	75 g
Fibres	19 g
Fer	13 mg
Calcium	300 mg
Sodium	20 mg

Légumineuses nature

STÉRILISATION

QUANTITÉ TOTALE • 4 LITRES (16 TASSES)

À l'autoclave

Taille des pots	Temps de stérilisation
125 ml (4 oz)	65 minutes
250 ml (8 oz)	65 minutes
500 ml (16 oz)	65 minutes
1 litre (32 oz)	75 minutes

Préparation
5 minutes

Trempage
12 heures

Cuisson
5 minutes

- **sans œuf**
- **sans produits laitiers**
- **sans noix**
- **végé**
- **sans gluten**

1 kg (environ 2 ¼ lb) de légumineuses sèches au choix (voir encadré ci-dessous)

1. La veille, bien rincer les légumineuses à l'eau froide à l'aide d'une passoire fine. Déposer les légumineuses dans un très grand bol rempli de 2,5 litres (10 tasses) d'eau froide. Laisser tremper au frais toute une nuit (de 12 à 18 heures).

2. Au moment de la cuisson, égoutter les légumineuses et jeter l'eau de trempage. Rincer de nouveau les légumineuses à l'eau froide.

3. Verser les légumineuses dans une grande casserole en acier inoxydable et couvrir d'eau froide. Porter à ébullition. Dès les premiers frémissements, retirer du feu.

4. À l'aide d'une cuillère trouée, répartir les légumineuses dans les pots en les remplissant aux trois quarts.

5. Couvrir les légumineuses d'eau de cuisson (ou d'eau bouillante propre), en laissant un espace libre de 2,5 cm (1 po) entre l'eau et le rebord des pots.

6. Plonger un ustensile dans les pots et le remuer afin d'éliminer toute bulle d'air. Au besoin, ajouter de l'eau.

7. Stériliser à l'autoclave (65 minutes pour des pots de 125 ml, de 250 ml ou de 500 ml, et 75 minutes pour des pots de 1 litre) selon les indications de la page 20.

Quelles légumineuses utiliser ?

On peut mettre presque toutes les légumineuses en conserves, et on peut même combiner plusieurs sortes pour avoir un mélange tout prêt pour les salades. Évitez toutefois les gourganes, les lentilles corail, les haricots roses, les doliques à œil noir ou les autres légumineuses à cuisson rapide. Parmi les légumineuses qui conviennent particulièrement bien à la mise en conserve, on trouve les pois chiches, les haricots pinto, les haricots *navy* et les haricots noirs.

PAR PORTION 1 pot de 500 ml	
Calories	546
Protéines	73 g
M.G.	26 g
Glucides	1 g
Fibres	0 g
Fer	7 mg
Calcium	31 mg
Sodium	756 mg

Cubes de bœuf nature

STÉRILISATION

QUANTITÉ TOTALE • 1,5 LITRE (6 TASSES)

À l'autoclave

Taille des pots	Temps de stérilisation
250 ml (8 oz)	65 minutes
500 ml (16 oz)	75 minutes
1 litre (32 oz)	90 minutes

Préparation
15 minutes

Cuisson
10 minutes

- **sans œuf**
- **sans produits laitiers**
- **sans noix**

1 kg (environ 2 ¼ lb) de cubes de bœuf coupés en cubes de 2,5 cm (1 po)

500 ml (2 tasses) de bouillon au choix (voir recettes aux pages 30, 32 et 40)

1. Dans une grande poêle antiadhésive, faire dorer les cubes de bœuf sur toutes les faces à feu élevé.

2. Répartir le bœuf dans les bocaux, en laissant un espace libre de 2,5 cm (1 po) entre le bœuf et le rebord des pots.

3. Dans une casserole en acier inoxydable, porter le bouillon à ébullition.

4. Verser le bouillon bouillant dans les bocaux, en laissant un espace libre de 2,5 cm (1 po) entre le bouillon et le rebord des pots.

5. Plonger un ustensile dans les pots et le remuer afin d'éliminer toute bulle d'air. Au besoin, ajouter du bouillon.

6. Stériliser à l'autoclave (65 minutes pour des pots de 250 ml, 75 minutes pour des pots de 500 ml et 90 minutes pour des pots de 1 litre) selon les indications de la page 20.

Dinde congelée et son bouillon

PAR PORTION 1 pot de 1 litre (bouillon seulement)	
Calories	123
Protéines	26 g
M.G.	4 g
Glucides	1 g
Fibres	0 g
Fer	1 mg
Calcium	14 mg
Sodium	55 mg

STÉRILISATION

À l'autoclave

QUANTITÉ TOTALE • 2 LITRES (8 TASSES) DE VIANDE ET 7 LITRES (28 TASSES) DE BOUILLON

Taille des pots	Temps de stérilisation de la viande	Temps de stérilisation du bouillon
250 ml (8 oz)	65 minutes	–
500 ml (16 oz)	75 minutes	25 minutes
1 litre (32 oz)	90 minutes	35 minutes

PAR PORTION 1 pot de 1 litre (viande et bouillon)	
Calories	2062
Protéines	459 g
M.G.	73 g
Glucides	1 g
Fibres	0 g
Fer	9 mg
Calcium	128 mg
Sodium	920 mg

Préparation
15 minutes

Temps de repos
3 heures

Cuisson
30 minutes

- **sans œuf**
- **sans produits laitiers**
- **sans noix**
- **sans gluten**

1 dinde entière congelée de 4,5 kg (10 lb)

330 ml (1 ⅓ tasse) d'oignons coupés en quartiers (227 g)

250 ml (1 tasse) de carottes avec les fanes coupées en morceaux (135 g)

160 ml (⅔ de tasse) de céleri avec les feuilles coupé en morceaux (80 g)

30 ml (2 c. à soupe) de persil séché

10 grains de poivre (ou plus, au goût)

4 grosses gousses d'ail (28 g)

1 feuille de laurier

Sel au goût

1. Sur la grille du fond de l'autoclave, déposer la dinde. Ajouter le reste des ingrédients.

2. Verser de l'eau jusqu'aux deux tiers de la cuve de l'autoclave, puis visser le couvercle. Allumer le feu à élevé et placer la pesée de 15 psi sur la soupape d'évacuation (peu importe l'altitude). Il n'est pas nécessaire de laisser l'autoclave ventiler 10 minutes s'il sert pour la cuisson plutôt que pour la stérilisation.

3. À partir du moment où la pesée se met à bouger, cuire 30 minutes, en s'assurant de maintenir la pression à 15 psi.

4. Éteindre le feu et laisser la chaleur et la pression retomber d'elles-mêmes.

5. Retirer la dinde de l'autoclave et la réserver dans une assiette.

6. À l'aide d'une passoire fine, filtrer le bouillon contenu dans l'autoclave au-dessus d'un grand bol, puis le laisser reposer de 3 à 4 heures au frais, jusqu'à ce que le gras fige à la surface (cela peut être dehors si la température est froide). Jeter les légumes et les fines herbes.

7. Désosser la dinde, puis la défaire en morceaux.

8. Répartir la dinde dans les bocaux, en laissant un espace libre de 2,5 cm (1 po) entre la viande et le rebord des pots.

9. Retirer le gras à la surface du bouillon à l'aide d'une cuillère.

10. Verser le bouillon dans une casserole en acier inoxydable et porter à ébullition. Goûter et rectifier l'assaisonnement au besoin. Si désiré, il est possible de faire réduire le bouillon davantage pour concentrer les saveurs.

11. Verser le bouillon bouillant dans les bocaux, en laissant un espace libre de 2,5 cm (1 po) entre le bouillon et le rebord des pots.

12. Plonger un ustensile dans les pots et le remuer afin d'éliminer toute bulle d'air. Au besoin, ajouter du bouillon.

13. Stériliser les pots de viande à l'autoclave (65 minutes pour des pots de 250 ml, 75 minutes pour des pots de 500 ml ou 90 minutes pour des pots de 1 litre) et les pots de bouillon (25 minutes pour des pots de 500 ml et 35 minutes pour des pots de 1 litre) selon les indications de la page 20.

Important

Plus la dinde est grosse, plus le temps de cuisson sera long. De plus, il faut se limiter à une dinde de 15 lb pour éviter de bloquer la soupape d'évacuation de l'autoclave (ce qui pourrait être dangereux, car la dinde gonfle pendant la cuisson dans l'autoclave).

Dinde de 10 à 11 lb (de 4,5 à 4,9 kg)	**30 minutes de cuisson**
Dinde de 12 à 13 lb (de 5 à 5,9 kg)	**45 minutes de cuisson**
Dinde de 14 à 15 lb (de 6 à 6,8 kg)	**90 minutes de cuisson**

PAR PORTION 15 ml (1 c. à soupe)	
Calories	16
Protéines	0 g
M.G.	0 g
Glucides	4 g
Fibres	1 g
Fer	1 mg
Calcium	20 mg
Sodium	851 mg

Mélange d'épices jerk

Préparation
5 minutes

Quantité
1 pot de 250 ml (8 oz)

- **sans œuf**
- **sans produits laitiers**
- **sans noix**
- **végé**
- **sans gluten**

30 ml (2 c. à soupe) de sel

30 ml (2 c. à soupe) de poudre d'oignon

30 ml (2 c. à soupe) de piment de la Jamaïque (quatre-épices) moulu

15 ml (1 c. à soupe) de piment de Cayenne

15 ml (1 c. à soupe) de flocons de piment

15 ml (1 c. à soupe) de poudre d'ail

15 ml (1 c. à soupe) de thym séché

15 ml (1 c. à soupe) de persil séché

15 ml (1 c. à soupe) de sucre

15 ml (1 c. à soupe) de poivre

7,5 ml (½ c. à soupe) de muscade

5 ml (1 c. à thé) de cannelle

1. Dans un bol, mélanger les ingrédients du mélange d'épices.

2. Transvider le mélange d'épices dans un contenant hermétique de 250 ml (1 tasse). Ce mélange se conserve jusqu'à douze mois à température ambiante.

PAR PORTION 15 ml (1 c. à soupe)	
Calories	10
Protéines	1 g
M.G.	0 g
Glucides	2 g
Fibres	1 g
Fer	1 mg
Calcium	16 mg
Sodium	74 mg

Mélange d'épices indien

Préparation
5 minutes

Quantité
1 pot de 250 ml (8 oz)

- **sans œuf**
- **sans produits laitiers**
- **sans noix**
- **végé**
- **sans gluten**

45 ml (3 c. à soupe) de grains de coriandre moulus

45 ml (3 c. à soupe) de cumin

30 ml (2 c. à soupe) de piment de Cayenne

10 ml (2 c. à thé) de grains de fenugrec moulus

7,5 ml (½ c. à soupe) de poivre

5 ml (1 c. à thé) de clous de girofle moulus

5 ml (1 c. à thé) de grains de fenouil moulus

5 ml (1 c. à thé) de flocons de piment

5 ml (1 c. à thé) de moutarde en poudre

5 ml (1 c. à thé) de poudre d'ail

2,5 ml (½ c. à thé) de cannelle

2,5 ml (½ c. à thé) de curcuma

2,5 ml (½ c. à thé) de muscade

2,5 ml (½ c. à thé) de sel

1. Dans un bol, mélanger les ingrédients du mélange d'épices.

2. Transvider le mélange d'épices dans un contenant hermétique de 250 ml (1 tasse). Ce mélange se conserve jusqu'à douze mois à température ambiante.

PAR PORTION 15 ml (1 c. à soupe)	
Calories	20
Protéines	1 g
M.G.	1 g
Glucides	4 g
Fibres	1 g
Fer	1 mg
Calcium	24 mg
Sodium	891 mg

Mélange d'épices mexicain

Préparation
5 minutes

Quantité
1 pot de 250 ml (8 oz)

- **sans œuf**
- **sans produits laitiers**
- **sans noix**
- **végé**
- **sans gluten**

45 ml (3 c. à soupe) de poudre de chili

30 ml (2 c. à soupe) de cumin

30 ml (2 c. à soupe) de paprika

30 ml (2 c. à soupe) de sel

30 ml (2 c. à soupe) d'origan séché

30 ml (2 c. à soupe) de poudre d'oignon

30 ml (2 c. à soupe) de poudre d'ail

15 ml (1 c. à soupe) de poivre

5 ml (1 c. à thé) de sucre

1. Dans un bol, mélanger les ingrédients du mélange d'épices.

2. Transvider le mélange d'épices dans un contenant hermétique de 250 ml (1 tasse). Ce mélange se conserve jusqu'à douze mois à température ambiante.

PAR PORTION 15 ml (1 c. à soupe)	
Calories	16
Protéines	1 g
M.G.	0 g
Glucides	3 g
Fibres	1 g
Fer	1 mg
Calcium	42 mg
Sodium	865 mg

Mélange d'épices cajun

Préparation
5 minutes

Quantité
1 pot de 250 ml (8 oz)

- **sans œuf**
- **sans produits laitiers**
- **sans noix**
- **végé**
- **sans gluten**

60 ml (¼ de tasse) de basilic séché

60 ml (¼ de tasse) de poudre d'oignon

30 ml (2 c. à soupe) de sel

30 ml (2 c. à soupe) de piment de Cayenne

15 ml (1 c. à soupe) de poivre

15 ml (1 c. à soupe) de piment de la Jamaïque (quatre-épices) moulu

15 ml (1 c. à soupe) de poudre de chili

10 ml (2 c. à thé) de thym séché

10 ml (2 c. à thé) de moutarde en poudre

10 ml (2 c. à thé) de clous de girofle moulus

10 ml (2 c. à thé) de poudre d'ail

1. Dans un bol, mélanger les ingrédients du mélange d'épices.

2. Transvider le mélange d'épices dans un contenant hermétique de 250 ml (1 tasse). Ce mélange se conserve jusqu'à douze mois à température ambiante.

Fait maison

En plus d'être parfois coûteux, trop salés et pas très santé, les mélanges tout prêts d'herbes et d'épices vendus en épicerie peuvent contenir des ingrédients qui ne font pas bon ménage avec la mise en conserve maison. Je vous propose donc quelques mélanges à faire soi-même à la maison, ce qui vous permettra en plus d'ajuster les saveurs (et le piquant!) selon vos goûts.

TOMATES

Impossible de parler de conserves sans parler de tomates ! Laissez de côté les tomates en conserve du commerce et cuisinez mes recettes pour savourer des tomates fraîches en tout temps. Dans cette section, je vous fais part de mes recettes les plus convoitées, afin que vous puissiez déguster vos tomates à l'année !

Bœuf aux tomates et chou

PAR PORTION 1 pot de 500 ml	
Calories	367
Protéines	27 g
M.G.	19 g
Glucides	26 g
Fibres	7 g
Fer	6 mg
Calcium	126 mg
Sodium	325 mg

STÉRILISATION

QUANTITÉ TOTALE • 6 LITRES (24 TASSES)

Taille des pots	Temps de stérilisation
250 ml (8 oz)	65 minutes
500 ml (16 oz)	75 minutes
1 litre (32 oz)	90 minutes

À l'autoclave

Préparation
40 minutes

Cuisson
25 minutes

- **sans produits laitiers**
- **sans œuf**
- **sans noix**

30 ml (2 c. à soupe) d'huile végétale

750 ml (3 tasses) d'oignons hachés (420 g)

1,35 kg (3 lb) de bœuf haché

15 ml (1 c. à soupe) de sauce soya

15 ml (1 c. à soupe) de sauce Worcestershire

1,4 kg (3 lb) de chou vert coupé en lanières de 1 cm – ½ po

6 gousses d'ail hachées (30 g)

3 litres (12 tasses) de coulis de tomates (voir recette à la page 28)

30 ml (2 c. à soupe) de persil séché

30 ml (2 c. à soupe) de thym séché

15 ml (1 c. à soupe) de sauce piquante (facultatif)

10 ml (2 c. à thé) de gros sel

5 ml (1 c. à thé) de piment de la Jamaïque (quatre-épices) moulu

Poivre au goût

1. Dans une grande casserole en acier inoxydable, chauffer l'huile à feu moyen-élevé. Cuire les oignons et le bœuf haché de 10 à 12 minutes en égrainant la viande à l'aide d'une cuillère en bois, jusqu'à ce qu'elle ait perdu sa teinte rosée.

2. Déglacer avec la sauce soya et la sauce Worcestershire, en raclant le fond de la casserole avec une cuillère en bois afin de détacher les sucs de cuisson.

3. Réduire le feu à moyen, puis ajouter le chou et l'ail. Cuire 10 minutes, jusqu'à ce que le chou soit tombé.

4. Ajouter le reste des ingrédients. Porter à ébullition, puis laisser mijoter 5 minutes. Goûter et rectifier l'assaisonnement au besoin.

5. Répartir la préparation bouillante dans les bocaux, en laissant un espace libre de 2,5 cm (1 po) entre la préparation et le rebord des pots.

6. Plonger un ustensile dans les pots et le remuer afin d'éliminer toute bulle d'air. Au besoin, ajouter de la préparation.

7. Stériliser à l'autoclave (65 minutes pour des pots de 250 ml, 75 minutes pour des pots de 500 ml et 90 minutes pour des pots de 1 litre) selon les indications de la page 20.

! Cette recette est une version déconstruite des traditionnels cigares au chou. Je la sers sur du riz ou avec une purée de pommes de terre.

PAR PORTION 1 pot de 500 ml	
Calories	307
Protéines	49 g
M.G.	9 g
Glucides	24 g
Fibres	6 g
Fer	4 mg
Calcium	80 mg
Sodium	755 mg

Préparation à fajitas

STÉRILISATION

À l'autoclave

QUANTITÉ TOTALE • 6 LITRES (24 TASSES)

Taille des pots	Temps de stérilisation
250 ml (8 oz)	65 minutes
500 ml (16 oz)	75 minutes
1 litre (32 oz)	90 minutes

Préparation
10 minutes

Cuisson
5 minutes

- **sans produits laitiers**
- **sans œuf**
- **sans noix**

6 gousses d'ail hachées (30 g)

4 poivrons coupés en lanières (1,2 kg)

2 gros oignons coupés en tranches (280 g)

3 litres (12 tasses) de coulis de tomates (voir recette à la page 28)

3 litres (12 tasses) de dinde cuite (4 lb) effilochée (voir recette à la page 40)

125 ml (½ tasse) de mélange d'épices mexicain (voir recette à la page 44)

60 ml (¼ de tasse) de jus de citron

Sauce piquante au goût

Sel et poivre au goût

1. Dans une grande casserole en acier inoxydable, déposer tous les ingrédients. Porter à ébullition, puis laisser mijoter 5 minutes à feu moyen. Goûter et rectifier l'assaisonnement au besoin.

2. Répartir la préparation bouillante dans les bocaux, en laissant un espace libre de 2,5 cm (1 po) entre la préparation et le rebord des pots.

3. Plonger un ustensile dans les pots et le remuer afin d'éliminer toute bulle d'air. Au besoin, ajouter de la préparation.

4. Stériliser à l'autoclave (65 minutes pour des pots de 250 ml, 75 minutes pour des pots de 500 ml et 90 minutes pour des pots de 1 litre) selon les indications de la page 20.

PAR PORTION 1 pot de 500 ml	
Calories	190
Protéines	8 g
M.G.	3 g
Glucides	37 g
Fibres	10 g
Fer	6 mg
Calcium	129 mg
Sodium	655 mg

Salsa *Paradise*

STÉRILISATION

À la casserole

QUANTITÉ TOTALE • 11 LITRES (44 TASSES)

Taille des pots	Temps de stérilisation
125 ml (4 oz)	15 minutes
250 ml (8 oz)	15 minutes
500 ml (16 oz)	15 minutes
1 litre (32 oz)	15 minutes

Préparation
1 heure

Cuisson
16 minutes

- **végé**
- **sans produits laitiers**
- **sans œuf**
- **sans noix**
- **sans gluten**

10 litres (40 tasses) de coulis de tomates (voir recette à la page 28)

500 ml (2 tasses) de piments bananes coupés en dés (200 g)

1,5 litre (6 tasses) de poivrons rouges et jaunes coupés en dés (840 g)

2,25 litres (9 tasses) d'oignons coupés en dés (1,26 kg)

1,25 litre (5 tasses) de céleri avec les feuilles coupé en dés (700 g)

1 grosse tête d'ail hachée (84 g)

1,25 litre (5 tasses) de vinaigre blanc à 5 % d'acide acétique

75 ml (5 c. à soupe) de grains de moutarde

90 ml (6 c. à soupe) de gros sel (au goût)

45 ml (3 c. à soupe) de grains de cumin

1 litre (4 tasses) de persil plat frais (95 g)

500 ml (2 tasses) de coriandre fraîche (60 g)

125 ml (½ tasse) d'origan séché

250 ml (1 tasse) de jus de citron en bouteille

45 ml (3 c. à soupe) de sauce piquante de type Tabasco ou Frank's Red Hot (au goût, facultatif)

1. Dans une grande casserole en acier inoxydable, porter le coulis de tomates à ébullition à feu moyen.

2. Ajouter les piments bananes, les poivrons, les oignons, le céleri, l'ail, le vinaigre, les grains de moutarde et le gros sel, puis laisser mijoter 10 minutes.

3. Pendant ce temps, faire rôtir les grains de cumin dans une petite poêle 1 minute, afin qu'ils dégagent leurs arômes.

4. Dans le contenant du robot culinaire, mélanger les grains de cumin rôtis avec le persil, la coriandre, l'origan, le jus de citron et, si désiré, la sauce piquante. Mélanger jusqu'à l'obtention d'une texture de purée.

5. Ajouter la préparation aux fines herbes dans la casserole. Laisser mijoter 5 minutes à feu moyen pour des légumes plus croquants ou jusqu'à 30 minutes pour des légumes plus tendres et un mélange plus homogène.

6. Répartir la salsa bouillante dans les bocaux, en laissant un espace libre de 1 cm (½ po) entre la salsa et le rebord des pots.

7. Plonger un ustensile dans les pots et le remuer afin d'éliminer toute bulle d'air. Au besoin, ajouter de la salsa.

8. Stériliser à la casserole 15 minutes (pour des pots de 125 ml, de 250 ml, de 500 ml ou de 1 litre) selon les indications de la page 19.

! Cette salsa est plutôt douce et conviendra à la majorité des palais. On peut cependant contrôler l'intensité de son goût piquant en ajoutant ou non la sauce piquante dans la recette, mais aussi en modifiant les quantités de piments bananes et de poivrons qu'elle renferme. L'important, c'est d'avoir 2 litres (8 tasses) de piments et de poivrons au total, donc choisissez les quantités qui vous donneront l'équilibre parfait!

Sauce à pizza

PAR PORTION 1 pot de 500 ml	
Calories	311
Protéines	13 g
M.G.	5 g
Glucides	65 g
Fibres	16 g
Fer	15 mg
Calcium	350 mg
Sodium	1446 mg

STÉRILISATION

QUANTITÉ TOTALE • 6 LITRES (24 TASSES)

Taille des pots	Temps de stérilisation
125 ml (4 oz)	30 minutes
250 ml (8 oz)	30 minutes
500 ml (16 oz)	30 minutes
1 litre (32 oz)	30 minutes

Préparation
20 minutes

Cuisson
41 minutes

- **végé**
- **sans produits laitiers**
- **sans œuf**
- **sans noix**
- **sans gluten**

30 ml (2 c. à soupe) d'huile végétale

8 oignons hachés (1,12 kg)

6 têtes d'ail hachées (360 g)

8 feuilles de laurier émiettées

7,5 litres (30 tasses) de coulis de tomates (voir recette à la page 28)

125 ml (½ tasse) de sambal oelek

30 ml (2 c. à soupe) de sel

Poivre au goût

1 litre (4 tasses) de persil frais haché (95 g)

125 ml (½ tasse) de basilic séché (18 g)

125 ml (½ tasse) d'origan séché (16 g)

125 ml (½ tasse) de thym séché (16 g)

125 ml (½ tasse) de romarin séché (16 g)

180 ml (¾ de tasse) de jus de citron en bouteille

1. Dans une grande casserole en acier inoxydable, chauffer l'huile à feu moyen. Cuire les oignons 5 minutes.

2. Ajouter l'ail et cuire 1 minute.

3. Ajouter les feuilles de laurier, le coulis, le sambal oelek, le sel et le poivre. Remuer, puis laisser mijoter 30 minutes.

4. Ajouter les fines herbes et poursuivre la cuisson 5 minutes. Goûter et rectifier l'assaisonnement au besoin.

5. Si désiré, réduire la préparation en une purée lisse à l'aide d'un mélangeur à main.

6. Verser 3,75 ml (¼ de c. à soupe) de jus de citron dans chaque pot de 125 ml, 7,5 ml (½ c. à soupe) dans chaque pot de 250 ml, 15 ml (1 c. à soupe) dans chaque pot de 500 ml ou 30 ml (2 c. à soupe) dans chaque pot de 1 litre.

7. Répartir la sauce dans les bocaux, en laissant un espace libre de 1 cm (½ po) entre la sauce et le rebord des pots.

8. Plonger un ustensile dans les pots et le remuer afin d'éliminer toute bulle d'air. Au besoin, ajouter de la sauce.

9. Stériliser à la casserole 30 minutes (pour des pots de 125 ml, de 250 ml, de 500 ml ou de 1 litre) selon les indications de la page 19.

PAR PORTION 1 pot de 250 ml	
Calories	587
Protéines	4 g
M.G.	58 g
Glucides	18 g
Fibres	6 g
Fer	3 mg
Calcium	76 mg
Sodium	21 mg

Tomates confites dans l'huile de Julie

STÉRILISATION

QUANTITÉ TOTALE • 500 ML (2 TASSES)

Taille des pots	Temps de stérilisation
125 ml (4 oz)	15 minutes
250 ml (8 oz)	15 minutes

Préparation
10 minutes

Temps de repos
2 heures

Cuisson
4 heures

- **végé**
- **sans produits laitiers**
- **sans œuf**
- **sans noix**
- **sans gluten**

1 contenant de tomates cerises de couleurs variées de 680 g, coupées en deux

90 ml (6 c. à soupe) de jus de citron en bouteille

Quelques feuilles de basilic frais hachées

4 branches de thym frais

Sel et poivre au goût

125 ml (½ tasse) d'huile d'olive

1 gousse d'ail coupée en deux sur la longueur (5 g)

1 petit piment thaï coupé en deux sur la longueur (facultatif)

1. Préchauffer le four à 90 °C (200 °F).

2. Déposer les tomates sur une plaque de cuisson, face coupée vers le haut.

3. Verser 30 ml (2 c. à soupe) de jus de citron sur les tomates, puis parsemer de basilic et de thym. Saler et poivrer. Cuire au four 2 heures. Retirer du four et laisser tiédir.

4. Pendant ce temps, déposer l'huile, l'ail et le piment dans une petite casserole en acier inoxydable. Porter à ébullition, puis éteindre le feu. Laisser infuser 2 heures.

5. Retirer l'ail et le piment de la casserole. Verser l'huile parfumée sur les tomates.

6. Remettre la plaque au four et poursuivre la cuisson 2 heures. Les tomates doivent être bien cuites, mais pas complètement desséchées. Le temps de cuisson pourrait varier selon le type de tomates utilisées et leur taux d'humidité.

7. Retirer la plaque du four, puis jeter les tiges de thym.

8. Verser 15 ml (1 c. à soupe) de jus de citron dans chaque pot de 125 ml ou 30 ml (2 c. à soupe) dans chaque pot de 250 ml.

9. À l'aide d'une cuillère trouée, répartir les tomates dans les bocaux, en laissant un espace libre de 1 cm (½ po) entre les tomates et le rebord des pots.

10. Verser l'huile chaude dans les bocaux, en laissant un espace libre de 0,5 cm (¼ de po) entre l'huile et le rebord des pots.

11. Plonger un ustensile dans les pots et le remuer afin d'éliminer toute bulle d'air. Au besoin, ajouter de l'huile.

12. Stériliser à la casserole 15 minutes (pour des pots de 125 ml ou de 250 ml) selon les indications de la page 19.

! Cette recette a été créée par Julie Demers. Elle m'avait envoyé un échantillon de sa recette pour que je puisse en vérifier le pH et la sécurité. Quand j'ai ouvert le pot, ça sentait tellement bon que je lui ai tout de suite demandé sa recette! Je sers ces tomates avec du pain grillé ou avec des fromages à l'apéro.

Soupe végé aux saveurs du Maroc

PAR PORTION 1 pot de 500 ml	
Calories	195
Protéines	10 g
M.G.	3 g
Glucides	35 g
Fibres	8 g
Fer	3 mg
Calcium	78 mg
Sodium	947 mg

STÉRILISATION

À l'autoclave

QUANTITÉ TOTALE • 7 LITRES (28 TASSES)

Taille des pots	Temps de stérilisation
500 ml (16 oz)	60 minutes
1 litre (32 oz)	75 minutes

Préparation
40 minutes

Cuisson
16 minutes

- **végé**
- **sans produits laitiers**
- **sans œuf**
- **sans noix**

125 ml (½ tasse) de riz sauvage rincé et égoutté (100 g)

250 ml (1 tasse) de haricots mungo rincés et égouttés (200 g)

250 ml (1 tasse) de lentilles du Puy rincées et égouttées (180 g)

30 ml (2 c. à soupe) d'huile végétale

2 oignons hachés (280 g)

1 contenant de champignons de Paris de 227 g, lavés et coupés en quartiers

3 carottes coupées en dés (280 g)

2 branches de céleri coupées en dés (140 g)

3 gousses d'ail hachées (15 g)

30 ml (2 c. à soupe) de mélange d'épices à couscous (voir encadré ci-dessous)

1 litre (4 tasses) de tomates coupées en dés ou de coulis de tomates (voir recette à la page 28)

5 litres (20 tasses) de bouillon de légumes (voir recette à la page 32)

60 ml (¼ de tasse) de jus de citron

Sel et poivre au goût

60 ml (¼ de tasse) de persil frais haché ou de coriandre fraîche hachée

1. Répartir le riz, les haricots et les lentilles dans les pots.

2. Dans une grande casserole en acier inoxydable, chauffer l'huile à feu moyen. Cuire les oignons et les champignons 5 minutes.

3. Ajouter les carottes et le céleri. Cuire 5 minutes.

4. Ajouter l'ail. Poursuivre la cuisson 1 minute.

5. Ajouter le reste des ingrédients. Porter à ébullition, puis laisser mijoter 5 minutes.

6. À l'aide d'une cuillère trouée, répartir les légumes dans les bocaux, en laissant un espace libre de 3 cm (1 ½ po) entre les légumes et le rebord des pots.

7. Verser le bouillon bouillant dans les bocaux, en laissant un espace libre de 2,5 cm (1 po) entre le bouillon et le rebord des pots.

8. Plonger un ustensile dans les pots et le remuer afin d'éliminer toute bulle d'air. Au besoin, ajouter du bouillon.

9. Stériliser à l'autoclave (60 minutes pour des pots de 500 ml et 75 minutes pour des pots de 1 litre) selon les indications de la page 20.

Ma recette de mélange d'épices à couscous

Dans un bol, mélanger 45 ml (3 c. à soupe) de cumin avec 30 ml (2 c. à soupe) de sel, 15 ml (1 c. à soupe) de gingembre moulu, 15 ml (1 c. à soupe) de poivre, 15 ml (1 c. à soupe) de cannelle, 15 ml (1 c. à soupe) de piment de Cayenne, 15 ml (1 c. à soupe) de grains de coriandre moulus, 10 ml (2 c. à thé) de clous de girofle moulus, 10 ml (2 c. à thé) de paprika et 10 ml (2 c. à thé) de curcuma. Transvider le mélange d'épices dans un contenant hermétique de 250 ml (1 tasse). Ce mélange se conserve jusqu'à douze mois à température ambiante.

PAR PORTION 1 pot de 250 ml	
Calories	132
Protéines	3 g
M.G.	1 g
Glucides	30 g
Fibres	4 g
Fer	2 mg
Calcium	100 mg
Sodium	42 mg

Ketchup à la rhubarbe

STÉRILISATION

QUANTITÉ TOTALE • 1 LITRE (4 TASSES)

Taille des pots	Temps de stérilisation
125 ml (4 oz)	15 minutes
250 ml (8 oz)	15 minutes
500 ml (16 oz)	15 minutes
1 litre (32 oz)	15 minutes

Préparation
20 minutes

Cuisson
1 heure

- **végé**
- **sans produits laitiers**
- **sans œuf**
- **sans noix**

500 ml (2 tasses) de rhubarbe pelée et coupée en tronçons de 1 cm – ½ po (260 g)

500 ml (2 tasses) de coulis de tomates (voir recette à la page 28)

250 ml (1 tasse) d'oignons coupés en dés (140 g)

180 ml (¾ de tasse) de pommes pelées et coupées en dés (110 g)

125 ml (½ tasse) de céleri coupé en dés (70 g)

125 ml (½ tasse) de vinaigre blanc à 5 % d'acide acétique

60 ml (¼ de tasse) de sucre (70 g)

1,25 ml (¼ de c. à thé) de piment de la Jamaïque (quatre-épices) moulu

1,25 ml (¼ de c. à thé) de flocons de piment

1,25 ml (¼ de c. à thé) de clous de girofle moulus

1,25 ml (¼ de c. à thé) de cannelle

0,625 ml (⅛ de c. à thé) de poivre

0,625 ml (⅛ de c. à thé) de muscade

0,625 ml (⅛ de c. à thé) de grains de coriandre moulus

0,625 ml (⅛ de c. à thé) de grains d'aneth moulus

1 feuille de laurier émiettée

Sel au goût

1. Dans une grande casserole en acier inoxydable, déposer tous les ingrédients. Porter à ébullition, puis laisser mijoter 1 heure à feu doux, en remuant de temps en temps. Goûter et rectifier l'assaisonnement au besoin.

2. Répartir le ketchup dans les bocaux, en laissant un espace libre de 0,5 cm (¼ de po) entre le ketchup et le rebord des pots.

3. Plonger un ustensile dans les pots et le remuer afin d'éliminer toute bulle d'air. Au besoin, ajouter du ketchup.

4. Stériliser à la casserole 15 minutes (pour des pots de 125 ml, de 250 ml, de 500 ml ou de 1 litre) selon les indications de la page 19.

! La rhubarbe pousse abondamment dans nos cours arrières, mais nous avons peu de recettes pour la cuisiner. Ce ketchup est comparable au ketchup aux fruits classique grâce aux épices qu'il contient. Il est possible de congeler la rhubarbe au printemps afin de faire la recette avec les tomates récoltées à l'automne, ou d'utiliser des tomates en conserve pour faire la recette avec la rhubarbe fraîche!

FRUITS

J'ai lu quelque part que les fruits sont les bonbons de la nature. Puisqu'ils sont naturellement sucrés, j'essaie d'ajouter le moins de sucre possible à mes cannages de fruits, voire de ne pas en mettre du tout. Il y a quand même des exceptions, puis qu'il faut bien se gâter parfois ! Dans cette section, découvrez des recettes à base de fruits à déguster sur un dessert, un bon fromage ou même à la cuillère !

PAR PORTION 1 pot de 250 ml de compote de pommes	
Calories	207
Protéines	1 g
M.G.	0 g
Glucides	55 g
Fibres	5 g
Fer	0 mg
Calcium	18 mg
Sodium	3 mg

Compote de fruits

STÉRILISATION

À la casserole

QUANTITÉ TOTALE • 1,75 LITRE (7 TASSES)

Taille des pots	Temps de stérilisation
125 ml (4 oz)	10 minutes
250 ml (8 oz)	10 minutes
500 ml (16 oz)	10 minutes
1 litre (32 oz)	10 minutes

Préparation
5 minutes

Cuisson
30 minutes

- sans œuf
- sans produits laitiers
- sans noix
- végé
- sans gluten

2 kg (environ 4 ½ lb) de fruits frais ou surgelés coupés en gros cubes, parmi les suivants :

- Abricots
- Bleuets
- Camerises
- Canneberges
- Cassis
- Fraises
- Framboises
- Kiwis
- Mangues
- Mûres
- Nectarines
- Pêches
- Poires
- Pommes

30 ml (2 c. à soupe) de jus de citron en bouteille

125 ml (½ tasse) de sucre, facultatif (110 g)

1,25 ml (¼ de c. à thé) de cannelle (ou autre arôme ou épice au goût, facultatif)

1. Dans une grande casserole en acier inoxydable, mélanger tous les ingrédients. Porter à ébullition, puis laisser mijoter 30 minutes à feu doux-moyen en remuant de temps en temps. Au besoin, ajouter 60 ml (¼ de tasse) d'eau dans la casserole, pour éviter que les fruits collent.

2. À l'aide du mélangeur à main ou dans le contenant du robot culinaire, broyer les fruits bouillis, jusqu'à l'obtention d'une texture lisse.

3. Répartir la compote bouillante dans les bocaux, en laissant un espace libre de 0,5 cm (¼ de po) entre la compote et le rebord des pots.

4. Plonger un ustensile dans les pots et le remuer afin d'éliminer toute bulle d'air. Au besoin, ajouter de la compote.

5. Stériliser à la casserole 10 minutes (pour des pots de 125 ml, de 250 ml, de 500 ml ou de 1 litre) selon les indications de la page 19.

!

On peut faire cette compote avec des fruits frais de saison, mais aussi avec des fruits un peu «fatigués», comme ceux qui ont passé une journée dans une boîte à lunch et qui ont des meurtrissures ou des fruits déclassés des marchés publics. On retire alors les parties abîmées avant de couper le fruit en gros cubes ou en quartiers. On conserve ces fruits dans un grand sac de congélation, et lorsque le sac est plein, on fait de la compote! J'essaie de garder les pelures comestibles des fruits autant que possible afin de conserver un maximum de fibres et de vitamines et pour donner une belle couleur à la compote.

PAR PORTION 1 pot de 500 ml	
Calories	683
Protéines	2 g
M.G.	1 g
Glucides	161 g
Fibres	9 g
Fer	1 mg
Calcium	46 mg
Sodium	0 mg

Poires au Grand Marnier

STÉRILISATION

QUANTITÉ TOTALE • 3 LITRES (12 TASSES)

Taille des pots	Temps de stérilisation
125 ml (4 oz)	10 minutes
250 ml (8 oz)	10 minutes
500 ml (16 oz)	10 minutes
1 litre (32 oz)	10 minutes

À la casserole

Préparation
15 minutes

Cuisson
1 minute

- **sans œuf**
- **sans produits laitiers**
- **sans noix**
- **végé**
- **sans gluten**

250 ml (1 tasse) de jus de citron en bouteille

5 ½ kg (12 lb) de poires mûres

Pour le sirop:

1,25 litre (5 tasses) d'eau

250 ml (1 tasse) de sucre (220 g)

250 ml (1 tasse) de liqueur d'agrumes de type Grand Marnier (au goût)

1. Dans un grand bol, mélanger environ 4 litres (16 tasses) d'eau avec le jus de citron.

2. Peler et couper les poires en retirant les cœurs et les queues. Déposer les poires dans l'eau citronnée au fur et à mesure pour éviter qu'elles s'oxydent.

3. Dans une grande casserole en acier inoxydable, mélanger l'eau pour le sirop avec le sucre et la liqueur d'agrumes. Porter à ébullition.

4. Égoutter les poires, puis les ajouter dans la casserole. Faire bouillir 30 secondes, puis retirer les poires de la casserole à l'aide d'une cuillère trouée.

5. Répartir les poires dans les bocaux, en laissant un espace libre de 1 cm (½ po) entre les poires et le rebord des pots.

6. Verser le sirop bouillant dans les bocaux, en laissant un espace libre de 0,5 cm (¼ de po) entre le sirop et le rebord des pots.

7. Plonger un ustensile dans les pots et le remuer afin d'éliminer toute bulle d'air. Au besoin, ajouter du sirop.

8. Stériliser à la casserole 10 minutes (pour des pots de 125 ml, de 250 ml, de 500 ml ou de 1 litre) selon les indications de la page 19.

Ma recette de croustade aux poires au Grand Marnier

Égoutter 1 litre (4 tasses) de conserves de poires au Grand Marnier et déposer les poires dans un plat de cuisson. Dans un bol, mélanger 250 ml (1 tasse) de beurre ramolli avec 250 ml (1 tasse) de farine, 250 ml (1 tasse) de cassonade, 250 ml (1 tasse) de flocons d'avoine, 1 pincée de sel et 1 pincée de cannelle. Répartir la préparation sur les poires. Cuire au four 40 minutes à 190 °C (375 °F). Servie bien chaude avec une boule de crème glacée, cette croustade est un de mes desserts favoris!

Confiture aux graines de chia

PAR PORTION 1 pot de 125 ml	
Calories	117
Protéines	3 g
M.G.	4 g
Glucides	23 g
Fibres	10 g
Fer	1 mg
Calcium	103 mg
Sodium	4 mg

STÉRILISATION

QUANTITÉ TOTALE • 625 ML (2 ½ TASSES)

Taille des pots	Temps de stérilisation
125 ml (4 oz)	10 minutes
250 ml (8 oz)	10 minutes
500 ml (16 oz)	10 minutes

À la casserole

Préparation
5 minutes

Cuisson
15 minutes

- sans œuf
- sans produits laitiers
- sans noix
- végé
- sans gluten

1,25 litre (5 tasses) de mûres, fraises, framboises et bleuets surgelés ou frais (600 g)

75 ml (5 c. à soupe) de graines de chia moulues

30 ml (2 c. à soupe) d'eau

15 ml (1 c. à soupe) de jus de citron en bouteille

15 ml (1 c. à soupe) de sucre (14 g), ou plus au goût (facultatif)

1. Dans une casserole en acier inoxydable, déposer tous les ingrédients. Porter à ébullition, puis laisser mijoter 15 minutes à feu doux.

2. Si désiré, écraser les fruits à l'aide d'une fourchette ou verser la préparation dans le contenant du robot culinaire et mélanger jusqu'à l'obtention de la texture souhaitée.

3. Répartir la confiture bouillante dans les bocaux, en laissant un espace libre de 0,5 cm (¼ de po) entre la confiture et le rebord des pots.

4. Plonger un ustensile dans les pots et le remuer afin d'éliminer toute bulle d'air. Au besoin, ajouter de la confiture.

5. Stériliser à la casserole 10 minutes (pour des pots de 125 ml, de 250 ml ou de 500 ml) selon les indications de la page 19.

Coulis de petits fruits

PAR PORTION 1 pot de 250 ml	
Calories	184
Protéines	3 g
M.G.	1 g
Glucides	44 g
Fibres	10 g
Fer	1 mg
Calcium	54 mg
Sodium	5 mg

STÉRILISATION

QUANTITÉ TOTALE • 500 ML (2 TASSES)

Taille des pots	Temps de stérilisation
125 ml (4 oz)	10 minutes
250 ml (8 oz)	10 minutes
500 ml (16 oz)	10 minutes
1 litre (32 oz)	10 minutes

À la casserole

Préparation
5 minutes

Cuisson
30 minutes

- **sans œuf**
- **sans produits laitiers**
- **sans noix**
- **végé**
- **sans gluten**

1,06 litre (4 ¼ tasses) de mûres, cerises et bleuets surgelés ou frais (600 g)

15 ml (1 c. à soupe) d'eau

15 ml (1 c. à soupe) de jus de citron en bouteille (facultatif)

15 ml (1 c. à soupe) de sucre (14 g), ou plus au goût (facultatif)

1,25 ml (¼ de c. à thé) d'extrait de vanille (ou autre arôme ou épice), ou plus au goût (facultatif)

1. Dans une casserole en acier inoxydable, déposer tous les ingrédients. Porter à ébullition, puis couvrir et laisser mijoter 15 minutes à feu doux.

2. Retirer le couvercle et poursuivre la cuisson 15 minutes.

3. Transvider la préparation dans le contenant du robot culinaire ou du mélangeur électrique. Mélanger jusqu'à l'obtention d'une texture lisse. Si désiré, filtrer le coulis à l'aide d'un tamis.

4. Répartir le coulis dans les bocaux, en laissant un espace libre de 0,5 cm (¼ de po) entre le coulis et le rebord des pots.

5. Plonger un ustensile dans les pots et le remuer afin d'éliminer toute bulle d'air. Au besoin, ajouter du coulis.

6. Stériliser à la casserole 10 minutes (pour des pots de 125 ml, de 250 ml, de 500 ml ou de 1 litre) selon les indications de la page 19.

! Cette recette est très polyvalente et peut être adaptée de plusieurs façons. L'eau sert à éviter que les fruits ne collent au fond de la casserole. Le jus de citron et le sucre donnent une texture un peu plus épaisse au coulis une fois celui-ci refroidi. Toutefois, vous pouvez omettre ces ingrédients ou en ajouter davantage, au goût. Pour cette recette, tous les petits fruits peuvent être utilisés: bleuets, fraises, framboises, mûres, cassis, camerises, canneberges, cerises, etc.

Pêches dans le sirop

PAR PORTION 1 pot de 250 ml	
Calories	346
Protéines	7 g
M.G.	2 g
Glucides	85 g
Fibres	15 g
Fer	2 mg
Calcium	46 mg
Sodium	0 mg

STÉRILISATION

QUANTITÉ TOTALE • 1,25 LITRE (5 TASSES)

Taille des pots	Temps de stérilisation
125 ml (4 oz)	10 minutes
250 ml (8 oz)	10 minutes
500 ml (16 oz)	10 minutes
1 litre (32 oz)	10 minutes

À la casserole

Préparation
20 minutes

Cuisson
30 minutes

- **sans œuf**
- **sans produits laitiers**
- **sans noix**
- **végé**
- **sans gluten**

250 ml (1 tasse) de jus de citron en bouteille

3 litres (12 tasses) de pêches (3,85 kg)

Pour le sirop :

600 ml (environ 2 ½ tasses) d'eau

70 ml (¼ de tasse + 2 c. à thé) de sucre (60 g)

1. Dans un grand bol, mélanger 2 litres (8 tasses) d'eau avec le jus de citron.

2. Peler les pêches et déposer les pelures dans une casserole en acier inoxydable.

3. Ajouter l'eau pour le sirop et le sucre dans la casserole. Porter à ébullition, puis laisser mijoter 30 minutes à feu doux. Retirer les pelures de pêches du sirop et les jeter.

4. Pendant ce temps, retirer le noyau des pêches et les couper en cubes. Déposer les cubes de pêches dans l'eau citronnée au fur et à mesure.

5. Égoutter les cubes de pêches, puis les ajouter dans la casserole. Porter de nouveau à ébullition, puis retirer du feu.

6. À l'aide d'une cuillère trouée, répartir les pêches dans les bocaux, en laissant un espace libre de 1 cm (½ po) entre les pêches et le rebord des pots.

7. Verser le sirop bouillant dans les bocaux, en laissant un espace libre de 0,5 cm (¼ de po) entre le sirop et le rebord des pots.

8. Plonger un ustensile dans les pots et le remuer afin d'éliminer toute bulle d'air. Au besoin, ajouter du sirop.

9. Stériliser à la casserole 10 minutes (pour des pots de 125 ml, de 250 ml, de 500 ml ou de 1 litre) selon les indications de la page 19.

! Les pêches à noyau non adhérent (Freestone) ont un noyau qui se détache plus facilement de la chair. Le fait d'infuser l'eau avec les pelures des pêches permet d'aromatiser le sirop et ainsi de réduire la quantité de sucre nécessaire. Si l'on n'infuse pas le sirop, les pêches perdront de leur saveur et leur goût sera très fade.

Confiture de canneberges, pommes et noix de coco

PAR PORTION 1 pot de 250 ml	
Calories	414
Protéines	3 g
M.G.	21 g
Glucides	61 g
Fibres	13 g
Fer	2 mg
Calcium	45 mg
Sodium	22 mg

STÉRILISATION

QUANTITÉ TOTALE • 750 ML (3 TASSES)

Taille des pots	Temps de stérilisation
125 ml (4 oz)	10 minutes
250 ml (8 oz)	10 minutes
500 ml (16 oz)	10 minutes

À la casserole

Préparation
10 minutes

Cuisson
20 minutes

- sans œuf
- sans produits laitiers
- sans noix
- végé
- sans gluten

1 litre (4 tasses) de canneberges fraîches ou surgelées (400 g)

375 ml (1 ½ tasse) de pommes pelées et coupées en petits dés (218 g)

250 ml (1 tasse) de noix de coco râpée (sucrée ou non, au goût)

180 ml (¾ de tasse) d'eau

125 ml (½ tasse) de cassonade, ou plus au goût (80 g)

1. Dans une casserole en acier inoxydable, déposer tous les ingrédients. Porter à ébullition, puis laisser mijoter 20 minutes à feu doux.

2. Répartir la confiture bouillante dans les pots, en laissant un espace libre de 0,5 cm (¼ de po) entre la confiture et le rebord des pots.

3. Plonger un ustensile dans les bocaux et le remuer afin d'éliminer toute bulle d'air. Au besoin, ajouter de la confiture.

4. Stériliser 10 minutes à la casserole (pour des pots de 125 ml, de 250 ml ou de 500 ml) selon les indications de la page 19.

! Cette recette surprenante me rappelle le Sud grâce à la noix de coco. Je l'aime sur des rôties, mais aussi sur un bon fromage à pâte molle comme le brie. Encore plus intéressant: je m'en sers comme base pour les cocktails, mélangée avec un bon rhum et allongée avec de l'eau pétillante!

Compote de rhubarbe, orange et gingembre

PAR PORTION 1 pot de 500 ml	
Calories	1031
Protéines	8 g
M.G.	2 g
Glucides	267 g
Fibres	22 g
Fer	4 mg
Calcium	567 mg
Sodium	30 mg

STÉRILISATION

QUANTITÉ TOTALE • 750 ML (3 TASSES)

Taille des pots	Temps de stérilisation
125 ml (4 oz)	10 minutes
250 ml (8 oz)	10 minutes
500 ml (16 oz)	10 minutes
1 litre (32 oz)	10 minutes

À la casserole

Préparation
20 minutes

Cuisson
40 minutes

- sans œuf
- sans produits laitiers
- sans noix
- végé
- sans gluten

1,5 litre (6 tasses) de rhubarbe pelée et coupée en tronçons de 1 cm – ½ po (1 kg)

4 oranges (960 g)

125 ml (½ tasse) de sucre (110 g)

250 ml (1 tasse) de miel

15 ml (1 c. à soupe) de gingembre râpé

1. Dans une casserole en acier inoxydable, déposer la rhubarbe.

2. Prélever le zeste d'une orange et l'ajouter dans la casserole.

3. Prélever les suprêmes des oranges en coupant d'abord l'écorce à vif, puis en tranchant de chaque côté des membranes. Déposer les suprêmes d'orange dans la casserole.

4. Ajouter le sucre, le miel et le gingembre. Porter à ébullition, puis laisser mijoter 40 minutes à feu doux en remuant de temps en temps.

5. Répartir la compote bouillante dans les bocaux, en laissant un espace libre de 0,5 cm (¼ de po) entre la compote et le rebord des pots.

6. Plonger un ustensile dans les pots et le remuer afin d'éliminer toute bulle d'air. Au besoin, ajouter de la compote.

7. Stériliser à la casserole 10 minutes (pour des pots de 125 ml, de 250 ml, de 500 ml ou de 1 litre) selon les indications de la page 19.

! Prélever les suprêmes d'orange peut être intimidant les premières fois. Pour vous aider, regardez des vidéos en ligne. L'objectif est de retirer le plus de membrane blanche possible, car elle peut donner un goût amer à la recette. Si votre compote est amère, vous pouvez y ajouter plus de sucre.

PAR PORTION 1 pot de 250 ml	
Calories	447
Protéines	5 g
M.G.	19 g
Glucides	68 g
Fibres	10 g
Fer	6 mg
Calcium	63 mg
Sodium	52 mg

Confiture choco-cerises

STÉRILISATION

QUANTITÉ TOTALE • 750 ML (3 TASSES)

Taille des pots	Temps de stérilisation
125 ml (4 oz)	10 minutes
250 ml (8 oz)	10 minutes

À la casserole

Préparation
20 minutes

Cuisson
20 minutes

- **sans œuf**
- **sans produits laitiers**
- **sans noix**
- **végé**
- **sans gluten**

1 litre (4 tasses) de cerises Bing équeutées, dénoyautées et coupées en deux (520 g)

30 ml (2 c. à soupe) d'eau

500 ml (2 tasses) de sucre (440 g)

130 g (environ ¼ de lb) de chocolat noir 70 % sans lactose

15 ml (1 c. à soupe) de jus de citron en bouteille

1 sachet de pectine en cristaux (57 g)

1. Dans une grande casserole en acier inoxydable, déposer les cerises, l'eau et le sucre. Porter à ébullition, puis laisser mijoter 10 minutes à feu doux en remuant, jusqu'à ce que le sucre soit complètement dissout.

2. Couper le chocolat en petits morceaux.

3. Ajouter le chocolat et le jus de citron dans la casserole. Remuer. Poursuivre la cuisson 10 minutes en remuant de temps en temps, jusqu'à ce que le chocolat ait complètement fondu.

4. Ajouter la pectine et porter à vive ébullition en remuant constamment pendant 1 minute.

5. Répartir la confiture bouillante dans les bocaux, en laissant un espace libre de 0,5 cm (¼ de po) entre la confiture et le rebord des pots.

6. Plonger un ustensile dans les pots et le remuer afin d'éliminer toute bulle d'air. Au besoin, ajouter de la confiture.

7. Stériliser à la casserole 10 minutes (pour des pots de 125 ml ou de 250 ml) selon les indications de la page 19.

!

La cerise est mon fruit préféré. Combinée au chocolat, elle crée ce qui est de loin ma confiture favorite. J'utilise des cerises surgelées quand les fraîches sont hors de prix ou lorsqu'elles ne sont pas en saison. Pour les amateurs de chocolat noir, n'hésitez pas à utiliser un chocolat à teneur plus élevée en cacao. Le goût du chocolat sera alors plus prononcé. Puisqu'il y a de la pectine dans cette recette, ne la doublez pas. Si vous en voulez plus, faites la recette une seconde fois.

Confiture
choco-cerise

Chutney de mangue épicé

PAR PORTION 1 pot de 250 ml	
Calories	326
Protéines	3 g
M.G.	10 g
Glucides	61 g
Fibres	4 g
Fer	1 mg
Calcium	39 mg
Sodium	6 mg

STÉRILISATION

À la casserole

QUANTITÉ TOTALE • 750 ML (3 TASSES)

Taille des pots	Temps de stérilisation
125 ml (4 oz)	10 minutes
250 ml (8 oz)	10 minutes
500 ml (16 oz)	10 minutes
1 litre (32 oz)	10 minutes

Préparation
20 minutes

Cuisson
35 minutes

- sans œuf
- sans produits laitiers
- sans noix
- végé
- sans gluten

30 ml (2 c. à soupe) d'huile végétale

60 ml (¼ de tasse) d'échalote sèche (française) hachée finement (35 g)

1 gousse d'ail hachée (5 g)

15 ml (1 c. à soupe) de gingembre haché (12 g)

2,5 ml (½ c. à thé) de grains de moutarde

1,25 ml (¼ de c. à thé) de cumin

0,625 ml (⅛ de c. à thé) de cannelle

0,625 ml (⅛ de c. à thé) de curcuma

1 piment thaï (5 g) haché (facultatif)

60 ml (¼ de tasse) de miel (70 g)

60 ml (¼ de tasse) de vinaigre blanc à 5 % d'acide acétique

1 litre (4 tasses) de mangues pelées et coupées en dés (680 g)

Sel et poivre au goût

1. Dans une casserole en acier inoxydable, chauffer l'huile à feu moyen.

2. Ajouter l'échalote, l'ail, le gingembre, les épices et, si désiré, le piment thaï dans la casserole. Cuire 5 minutes en remuant, jusqu'à l'obtention d'une pâte.

3. Ajouter le miel, le vinaigre et les mangues. Saler et poivrer. Laisser mijoter 30 minutes à feu doux en remuant de temps en temps.

4. Répartir le chutney bouillant dans les bocaux, en laissant un espace libre de 0,5 cm (¼ de po) entre le chutney et le rebord des pots.

5. Plonger un ustensile dans les pots et le remuer afin d'éliminer toute bulle d'air. Au besoin, ajouter du chutney.

6. Stériliser à la casserole 10 minutes (pour des pots de 125 ml, de 250 ml, de 500 ml ou de 1 litre) selon les indications de la page 19.

!

Cette recette d'inspiration indienne n'en finit plus de me surprendre. Sucré, salé, un peu vinaigré et épicé, ce chutney se prête bien aux plats indiens, mais il peut aussi être utilisé comme sauce pour les sautés, pour accompagner ou laquer les viandes, comme base de vinaigrette, et même sur des bagels avec du fromage à la crème. J'aime bien «rescaper» les mangues trop mûres en rabais à l'épicerie pour faire cette recette, mais des cubes de mangue surgelés feraient tout aussi bien l'affaire!

SAUCES

Condiment, accompagnement, assaisonnement : il s'agit souvent de la petite touche qui rend un plat ordinaire extraordinaire. Je vous propose des recettes de sauces allant de la sauce barbecue fumée aux pommes à la sauce pili-pili, qui me rappelle l'Inde et les Antilles.

PAR PORTION 1 pot de 125 ml	
Calories	190
Protéines	8 g
M.G.	10 g
Glucides	19 g
Fibres	6 g
Fer	1 mg
Calcium	107 mg
Sodium	104 mg

Houmous

STÉRILISATION

QUANTITÉ TOTALE • 625 ML (2 ½ TASSES)

Taille des pots	Temps de stérilisation
125 ml (4 oz)	10 minutes
250 ml (8 oz)	10 minutes

À la casserole

Préparation
5 minutes

Cuisson
2 minutes

- sans œuf
- sans produits laitiers
- végé
- sans gluten

500 ml (2 tasses) de pois chiches cuits (340 g)

250 ml (1 tasse) d'eau

90 ml (6 c. à soupe) de jus de citron en bouteille

90 ml (6 c. à soupe) de tahini (beurre de sésame)

2,5 ml (½ c. à thé) de cumin

2,5 ml (½ c. à thé) d'acide citrique en poudre

2 gousses d'ail (10 g)

Quelques gouttes de sauce piquante (facultatif)

Sel et poivre au goût

1. Dans une casserole en acier inoxydable, mélanger tous les ingrédients. Porter à ébullition, puis laisser mijoter 2 minutes à feu moyen.

2. Transvider la préparation dans le contenant du robot culinaire. Mélanger jusqu'à l'obtention d'une purée lisse.

3. Répartir le houmous chaud dans les bocaux (il est important que le houmous ne refroidisse pas trop avant la mise en pots), en laissant un espace libre de 0,25 cm (⅛ de po) entre le houmous et le rebord des pots.

4. Plonger un ustensile dans les pots et le remuer afin d'éliminer toute bulle d'air. Au besoin, ajouter du houmous.

5. Stériliser à la casserole 10 minutes (pour des pots de 125 ml ou de 250 ml) selon les indications de la page 19.

! L'ajout d'acide citrique est très important pour cette recette. On peut s'en procurer dans certaines pharmacies, dans les magasins d'aliments en vrac et dans les magasins d'aliments naturels. Il faut respecter les quantités d'ingrédients à la lettre pour s'assurer que le pH est assez bas.

PAR PORTION 1 pot de 125 ml	
Calories	450
Protéines	2 g
M.G.	23 g
Glucides	51 g
Fibres	2 g
Fer	1 mg
Calcium	81 mg
Sodium	13 mg

Confit d'oignons au porto

STÉRILISATION

QUANTITÉ TOTALE • 625 ML (2 ½ TASSES)

Taille des pots	Temps de stérilisation
125 ml (4 oz)	10 minutes
250 ml (8 oz)	10 minutes
500 ml (16 oz)	10 minutes

À la casserole

Préparation
5 minutes

Cuisson
1 heure
15 minutes

- **sans œuf**
- **sans produits laitiers**
- **sans noix**
- **végé**
- **sans gluten**

125 ml (½ tasse) d'huile végétale

1,33 litre (5 ⅓ tasses) d'oignons rouges coupés en demi-rondelles (900 g)

125 ml (½ tasse) de sirop d'érable

250 ml (1 tasse) de porto rouge

90 ml (6 c. à soupe) de vinaigre balsamique à minimum 5 % d'acide acétique

Sel et poivre au goût

1. Dans une poêle, chauffer l'huile à feu doux. Cuire les oignons et le sirop d'érable 15 minutes.

2. Ajouter le porto et le vinaigre balsamique. Saler et poivrer. Laisser mijoter 1 heure à feu doux, jusqu'à absorption presque complète du liquide.

3. Répartir le confit chaud dans les bocaux, en laissant un espace libre de 0,5 cm (¼ de po) entre le confit et le rebord des pots.

4. Plonger un ustensile dans les pots et le remuer afin d'éliminer toute bulle d'air. Au besoin, ajouter du confit.

5. Stériliser à la casserole 10 minutes (pour des pots de 125 ml, de 250 ml ou de 500 ml) selon les indications de la page 19.

Herbes salées

PAR PORTION 1 pot de 250 ml	
Calories	23
Protéines	1 g
M.G.	0 g
Glucides	5 g
Fibres	1 g
Fer	1 mg
Calcium	34 mg
Sodium	5367 mg

STÉRILISATION

QUANTITÉ TOTALE • 1,5 LITRE (6 TASSES)

Taille des pots	Temps de stérilisation
125 ml (4 oz)	10 minutes
250 ml (8 oz)	10 minutes
500 ml (16 oz)	10 minutes

À la casserole

Préparation
15 minutes

Temps de repos
14 heures

- sans œuf
- sans produits laitiers
- sans noix
- végé
- sans gluten

125 ml (½ tasse) de carotte coupée en tronçons (70 g)

250 ml (1 tasse) de céleri coupé en dés (138 g)

250 ml (1 tasse) de poireau émincé (90 g)

2 oignons verts hachés

80 ml (⅓ de tasse) de persil frais haché

60 ml (¼ de tasse) de ciboulette fraîche hachée

60 ml (¼ de tasse) d'aneth frais haché

15 ml (1 c. à soupe) de thym frais haché

30 ml (2 c. à soupe) de sel (28 g)

250 ml (1 tasse) de gros sel (286 g)

1. Dans le contenant du robot culinaire, déposer la carotte, le céleri et le poireau. Mélanger jusqu'à ce que les légumes soient hachés finement.

2. Dans un grand bol, mélanger les fines herbes avec les légumes hachés et le sel. Laisser reposer 2 heures au frais afin que la préparation dégorge.

3. À l'aide d'une passoire fine, retirer le plus d'eau possible de la préparation aux herbes.

5. Dans un autre bol, mélanger les herbes essorées avec le gros sel (la quantité de gros sel requise a été calculée selon la formule ci-dessous).

6. Répartir les herbes salées dans les bocaux, en laissant un espace libre de 0,5 cm (¼ de po) entre les herbes et le rebord des pots.

7. Déposer une grille au fond d'une casserole en acier inoxydable, puis y déposer les pots. Couvrir d'eau froide, exceptionnellement, et porter à ébullition. Dès que l'eau bout, stériliser 10 minutes (pour des pots de 125 ml, de 250 ml ou de 500 ml). Retirer les pots de la casserole et laisser reposer 12 heures.

!

$$\frac{\text{Poids des herbes x 40}}{60} = \text{poids du sel à ajouter}$$

Par exemple: mes herbes essorées pèsent 60 g. Je multiplie ce poids par 40 (ce qui donne 2400), et je divise cette valeur par 60. Ainsi, j'obtiens un total de 40 g de sel à ajouter à la recette.

Notez que pour éviter que la texture des herbes ne change et que ces dernières ne brunissent, le temps de stérilisation à l'eau bouillante a été réduit au minimum.

PAR PORTION 1 pot de 125 ml	
Calories	29
Protéines	1 g
M.G.	0 g
Glucides	7 g
Fibres	2 g
Fer	0 mg
Calcium	16 mg
Sodium	5 mg

Sauce piquante pili-pili

STÉRILISATION

QUANTITÉ TOTALE • 375 ML (1 ½ TASSE)

Taille des pots	Temps de stérilisation
125 ml (4 oz)	10 minutes
250 ml (8 oz)	10 minutes
500 ml (16 oz)	10 minutes

À la casserole

Préparation
10 minutes

Cuisson
15 minutes

- **sans œuf**
- **sans produits laitiers**
- **sans noix**
- **végé**
- **sans gluten**

250 ml (1 tasse) de piments piquants au choix, de style habanero ou jalapeño (150 g)

60 ml (¼ de tasse) de jus de citron en bouteille

2 gousses d'ail (10 g)

1 grosse tomate (200 g)

Sel au goût

1. À l'aide de gants, retirer les queues des piments et les déposer dans le contenant du robot culinaire. Ajouter le reste des ingrédients et donner quelques impulsions, jusqu'à ce que la préparation aux piments soit hachée finement.

2. Dans une casserole en acier inoxydable, verser la préparation aux piments. Porter à ébullition, puis laisser mijoter 15 minutes à feu moyen.

3. Répartir la sauce bouillante dans les bocaux, en laissant un espace libre de 0,5 cm (¼ de po) entre la sauce et le rebord des pots.

4. Plonger un ustensile dans les pots et le remuer afin d'éliminer toute bulle d'air. Au besoin, ajouter de la sauce.

5. Stériliser à la casserole 10 minutes (pour des pots de 125 ml, de 250 ml ou de 500 ml) selon les indications de la page 19.

! Ce sont la membrane et les graines des piments qui renferment le goût plus piquant: plus vous en conserverez, plus la sauce sera piquante! Si vous désirez obtenir une sauce qui ressemble davantage à un sambal oelek, remplacez le jus de citron par du vinaigre à 5% d'acide acétique.

PAR PORTION 1 pot de 250 ml	
Calories	137
Protéines	4 g
M.G.	8 g
Glucides	17 g
Fibres	4 g
Fer	3 mg
Calcium	51 mg
Sodium	46 mg

Sauce arrabbiata

STÉRILISATION

QUANTITÉ TOTALE • 1,5 LITRE (6 TASSES)

Taille des pots	Temps de stérilisation
250 ml (8 oz)	30 minutes
500 ml (16 oz)	30 minutes
1 litre (32 oz)	30 minutes

À l'autoclave

Préparation
15 minutes
Cuisson
13 minutes

- sans œuf
- sans produits laitiers
- sans noix
- végé
- sans gluten

45 ml (3 c. à soupe) d'huile d'olive

15 ml (1 c. à soupe) de flocons de piment (au goût)

250 ml (1 tasse) d'oignon haché finement (140 g)

6 gousses d'ail hachées (30 g)

1,5 litre (6 tasses) de coulis de tomates (voir recette à la page 28)

125 ml (½ tasse) de basilic frais haché grossièrement

Sel et poivre au goût

1. Dans une grande casserole en acier inoxydable, chauffer l'huile à feu moyen. Cuire les flocons de piment 2 minutes.

2. Ajouter l'oignon et poursuivre la cuisson 5 minutes.

3. Ajouter l'ail et poursuivre la cuisson 1 minute.

4. Ajouter le coulis de tomates et le basilic. Porter à ébullition, puis laisser mijoter 5 minutes à feu moyen en remuant. Goûter et rectifier l'assaisonnement au besoin.

5. Verser la sauce bouillante dans les bocaux, en laissant un espace libre de 1 cm (½ po) entre la sauce et le rebord des pots.

6. Plonger un ustensile dans les pots et le remuer afin d'éliminer toute bulle d'air. Au besoin, ajouter de la sauce.

7. Stériliser à l'autoclave 30 minutes (pour des pots de 250 ml, de 500 ml ou de 1 litre) selon les indications de la page 20.

Si vous utilisez des tomates fraîches, cette recette peut être préparée en même temps que le coulis de tomates de la page 28!

PAR PORTION 1 pot de 500 ml	
Calories	191
Protéines	4 g
M.G.	8 g
Glucides	30 g
Fibres	5 g
Fer	1 mg
Calcium	84 mg
Sodium	694 mg

Sauce à la courge

STÉRILISATION

QUANTITÉ TOTALE • 2 LITRES (8 TASSES)

Taille des pots	Temps de stérilisation
500 ml (16 oz)	55 minutes
1 litre (32 oz)	75 minutes

À l'autoclave

Préparation
20 minutes

Cuisson
30 minutes

- **sans œuf**
- **sans produits laitiers**
- **sans noix**
- **végé**
- **sans gluten**

1 litre (4 tasses) de courge Butternut ou de citrouille pelée et coupée en dés de 1 cm – ½ po (750 g)

250 ml (1 tasse) de courgette coupée en demi-rondelles de 1 cm – ½ po (180 g)

250 ml (1 tasse) d'oignon coupé en dés (140 g)

250 ml (1 tasse) de carotte coupée en rondelles de 1 cm – ½ po (140 g)

250 ml (1 tasse) de tomate coupée en dés (200 g)

1 gousse d'ail hachée (5 g)

30 ml (2 c. à soupe) d'huile végétale

1 piment thaï (5 g) haché finement (facultatif)

Sel et poivre au goût

1 litre (4 tasses) de bouillon de légumes (voir recette à la page 32)

125 ml (½ tasse) de bébés épinards bien tassés (50 g)

15 ml (1 c. à soupe) de pâte de cari verte

!

Voilà une belle recette pour éviter le gaspillage des citrouilles d'Halloween! Je sers cette sauce sur du riz ou avec des pâtes de farine de pois pour un repas plus protéiné, et j'y ajoute une grosse cuillerée de yogourt grec nature.

1. Préchauffer le four à 205 °C (400 °F).

2. Dans une grande casserole en acier inoxydable allant au four, déposer la courge ou la citrouille, la courgette, l'oignon, la carotte, la tomate, l'ail, l'huile et, si désiré, le piment thaï. Saler, poivrer et remuer. Cuire au four 30 minutes.

3. Retirer la casserole du four et la placer sur la cuisinière. Déglacer avec le bouillon à feu moyen, en raclant le fond de la casserole avec une cuillère en bois afin de détacher les sucs de cuisson.

4. Ajouter les épinards et la pâte de cari. Remuer et porter à ébullition. Goûter et rectifier l'assaisonnement au besoin.

5. À l'aide d'une cuillère trouée, répartir les aliments solides dans les bocaux, en laissant un espace libre de 2,5 cm (1 po) entre les aliments et le rebord des pots.

6. Verser le bouillon bouillant dans les bocaux, en laissant un espace libre de 2,5 cm (1 po) entre le bouillon et le rebord des pots.

7. Plonger un ustensile dans les pots et le remuer afin d'éliminer toute bulle d'air. Au besoin, ajouter du bouillon.

8. Stériliser à l'autoclave (55 minutes pour des pots de 500 ml et 75 minutes pour des pots de 1 litre) selon les indications de la page 20.

Sauce barbecue fumée aux pommes

PAR PORTION 1 pot de 250 ml	
Calories	215
Protéines	7 g
M.G.	2 g
Glucides	48 g
Fibres	7 g
Fer	4 mg
Calcium	76 mg
Sodium	1463 mg

STÉRILISATION

QUANTITÉ TOTALE • 1 LITRE (4 TASSES)

Taille des pots	Temps de stérilisation
125 ml (4 oz)	10 minutes
250 ml (8 oz)	10 minutes
500 ml (16 oz)	10 minutes
1 litre (32 oz)	10 minutes

À la casserole

Préparation
25 minutes

Cuisson
30 minutes

- **sans œuf**
- **sans produits laitiers**
- **sans noix**
- **végé**

1 boîte de pâte de tomates de 369 ml

500 ml (2 tasses) de compote de pommes

60 ml (¼ de tasse) de moutarde de Dijon

60 ml (¼ de tasse) de vinaigre de cidre de pomme à 5 % d'acide acétique

30 ml (2 c. à soupe) de sirop d'érable

30 ml (2 c. à soupe) de jus de citron en bouteille

30 ml (2 c. à soupe) de poudre d'oignon

15 ml (1 c. à soupe) de sauce piquante au choix (facultatif)

15 ml (1 c. à soupe) de vinaigre blanc à 5 % d'acide acétique

15 ml (1 c. à soupe) de sauce soya

15 ml (1 c. à soupe) de poudre d'ail

7,5 ml (½ c. à soupe) de sauce Worcestershire

2,5 ml (½ c. à thé) de poudre de chili

2,5 ml (½ c. à thé) de paprika fumé doux

2,5 ml (½ c. à thé) de poivre noir fraîchement moulu

1,25 ml (¼ de c. à thé) de fumée liquide

Sel au goût

1. Dans une grande casserole en acier inoxydable, mélanger tous les ingrédients. Porter à ébullition, puis laisser mijoter 30 minutes à feu doux.

2. Verser la sauce bouillante dans les bocaux, en laissant un espace libre de 0,5 cm (¼ de po) entre la sauce et le rebord des pots.

3. Plonger un ustensile dans les pots et le remuer afin d'éliminer toute bulle d'air. Au besoin, ajouter de la sauce.

4. Stériliser à la casserole 10 minutes (pour des pots de 125 ml, de 250 ml, de 500 ml ou de 1 litre) selon les indications de la page 19.

PAR PORTION 1 pot de 250 ml	
Calories	199
Protéines	4 g
M.G.	6 g
Glucides	36 g
Fibres	4 g
Fer	1 mg
Calcium	30 mg
Sodium	87 mg

Salsa de maïs

STÉRILISATION

QUANTITÉ TOTALE • 750 ML (3 TASSES)

Taille des pots	Temps de stérilisation
125 ml (4 oz)	10 minutes
250 ml (8 oz)	10 minutes
500 ml (16 oz)	10 minutes

À la casserole

Préparation
30 minutes

Cuisson
43 minutes

- **sans œuf**
- **sans produits laitiers**
- **sans noix**
- **végé**

500 ml (2 tasses) de maïs frais ou surgelé (280 g)

15 ml (1 c. à soupe) d'huile végétale

2,5 ml (½ c. à thé) de piment chile pasilla de Oaxaca en flocons ou de flocons de piment (facultatif)

5 ml (1 c. à thé) de mélange d'épices cajun (voir recette à la page 44)

3 gousses d'ail hachées (15 g)

80 ml (⅓ de tasse) de poivron rouge coupé en petits dés (45 g)

60 ml (¼ de tasse) de céleri coupé en petits dés (35 g)

80 ml (⅓ de tasse) d'oignon coupé en petits dés (50 g)

60 ml (¼ de tasse) de jalapeño coupé en petits dés (45 g)

160 ml (⅔ de tasse) de tomate coupée en petits dés (150 g)

125 ml (½ tasse) de vinaigre blanc à 5 % d'acide acétique

60 ml (¼ de tasse) de jus de citron en bouteille

30 ml (2 c. à soupe) de sucre (30 g)

15 ml (1 c. à soupe) de pâte de tomates

Sel et poivre au goût

1. Chauffer une poêle à feu moyen-élevé. Cuire le maïs de 5 à 7 minutes, jusqu'à ce qu'il soit légèrement doré.

2. Dans une casserole en acier inoxydable, chauffer l'huile à feu doux. Cuire le piment en flocons, les épices cajun et l'ail de 3 à 4 minutes en remuant, sans laisser l'ail colorer.

3. Ajouter le poivron, le céleri, l'oignon et le jalapeño. Bien mélanger et poursuivre la cuisson 5 minutes.

4. Ajouter le maïs et le reste des ingrédients. Bien mélanger. Couvrir et laisser mijoter 30 minutes à feu doux.

5. Verser la salsa bouillante dans les pots, en laissant un espace libre de 0,5 cm (¼ de po) entre la salsa et le rebord des pots.

6. Plonger un ustensile dans les pots et le remuer afin d'éliminer toute bulle d'air. Au besoin, ajouter de la salsa.

7. Stériliser à la casserole 10 minutes (pour des pots de 125 ml, de 250 ml ou de 500 ml) selon les indications de la page 19.

! Il est important de respecter les proportions de cette recette. Toutefois, il est possible d'omettre le jalapeño, ou de le remplacer par la même quantité de poivron doux. Les chiles séchés sont un élément essentiel de la cuisine mexicaine. On en trouve au Québec dans certaines boutiques spécialisées. Même en petite quantité, ils dévoilent une multitude de saveurs et de parfums. À essayer si vous en avez la chance! Cette salsa se déguste avec des croustilles de maïs ou en guise de garniture dans les tacos, sur la viande ou sur le poisson.

Bouillon pour fondue chinoise

PAR PORTION 1 pot de 500 ml	
Calories	219
Protéines	6 g
M.G.	11 g
Glucides	17 g
Fibres	2 g
Fer	1 mg
Calcium	58 mg
Sodium	1581 mg

STÉRILISATION

QUANTITÉ TOTALE • 7 LITRES (28 TASSES)

Taille des pots	Temps de stérilisation
500 ml (16 oz)	30 minutes
1 litre (32 oz)	40 minutes

À l'autoclave

Préparation
5 minutes

Cuisson
19 minutes

- **sans œuf**
- **sans produits laitiers**
- **sans noix**
- **sans gluten**

180 ml (¾ de tasse) d'huile végétale

1,66 litre (6 ⅔ tasses) d'oignons hachés finement (1 kg)

5 gousses d'ail hachées (25 g)

180 ml (¾ de tasse) de pâte de tomates

875 ml (3 ½ tasses) de vin blanc

6 litres (24 tasses) de bouillon de bœuf (voir recette à la page 30)

75 ml (5 c. à soupe) de sirop d'érable

75 ml (5 c. à soupe) de sauce soya

30 ml (2 c. à soupe) de sauce piquante au choix (facultatif)

30 ml (2 c. à soupe) de persil frais haché finement

4 feuilles de laurier émiettées

7 branches de thym effeuillées

Poivre au goût

1. Dans une grande casserole en acier inoxydable, chauffer l'huile à feu moyen. Cuire les oignons 5 minutes.

2. Ajouter l'ail et cuire 2 minutes.

3. Ajouter la pâte de tomates et poursuivre la cuisson 2 minutes en remuant.

4. Augmenter le feu à élevé et déglacer avec le vin blanc, en raclant le fond de la casserole avec une cuillère en bois afin de détacher les sucs de cuisson.

5. Réduire le feu à moyen et laisser mijoter 5 minutes, jusqu'à l'obtention d'une pâte un peu liquide.

6. Ajouter le reste des ingrédients dans la casserole et laisser mijoter 5 minutes. Goûter et rectifier l'assaisonnement au besoin.

7. Répartir le bouillon bouillant dans les bocaux, en laissant un espace libre de 2,5 cm (1 po) entre le bouillon et le rebord des pots.

8. Stériliser à l'autoclave (30 minutes pour des pots de 500 ml et 40 minutes pour des pots de 1 litre) selon les indications de la page 20.

MARINADES

Les marinades sont faites à partir d'aliments au pH élevé auxquels on ajoute un acidifiant pour en prolonger la conservation. Cette technique date de plusieurs milliers d'années. Autrefois préparées à partir d'un procédé de lactofermentation, les marinades sont de nos jours obtenues par l'ajout de vinaigre, de jus de citron en bouteille ou d'acide citrique. Ici, je vous fais découvrir mes meilleures recettes de légumes marinés.

PAR PORTION 1 pot de 250 ml	
Calories	154
Protéines	7 g
M.G.	1 g
Glucides	34 g
Fibres	2 g
Fer	2 mg
Calcium	187 mg
Sodium	18 mg

Ail haché en pot

STÉRILISATION

QUANTITÉ TOTALE • 250 ML (1 TASSE)

Taille des pots	Temps de stérilisation
125 ml (4 oz)	10 minutes
250 ml (8 oz)	10 minutes
500 ml (16 oz)	10 minutes

À la casserole

Préparation
15 minutes

- **sans œuf**
- **sans produits laitiers**
- **sans noix**
- **végé**
- **sans gluten**

80 ml (⅓ de tasse) d'eau

80 ml (⅓ de tasse) de jus de citron en bouteille

180 ml (¾ de tasse) d'ail haché (216 g)

1. Dans une casserole en acier inoxydable, mélanger l'eau avec le jus de citron. Porter à ébullition, puis ajouter l'ail. Retirer du feu.

2. Répartir l'ail dans les bocaux en pressant, puis couvrir de marinade bouillante, en laissant un espace libre de 0,5 cm (¼ de po) entre la marinade et le rebord des pots.

3. Plonger un ustensile dans les pots et le remuer afin d'éliminer toute bulle d'air. Au besoin, ajouter de la marinade.

4. Stériliser à la casserole 10 minutes (pour des pots de 125 ml, de 250 ml ou de 500 ml) selon les indications de la page 19.

! Attention! Il est important de choisir de l'ail frais, de préférence de saison, et qui n'a pas été réfrigéré. Lorsqu'il entre en contact avec du vinaigre, l'ail ayant été réfrigéré ou entreposé à moins de 6°C pourrait changer de couleur et devenir bleu-vert. Toutefois, notez que cette réaction enzymatique n'est pas dangereuse, et donc que l'ail ayant changé de couleur peut être consommé.

PAR PORTION 1 pot de 500 ml	
Calories	248
Protéines	7 g
M.G.	1 g
Glucides	51 g
Fibres	9 g
Fer	4 mg
Calcium	87 mg
Sodium	493 mg

Betteraves marinées

STÉRILISATION

QUANTITÉ TOTALE • 7,5 LITRES (30 TASSES)

Taille des pots	Temps de stérilisation
250 ml (8 oz)	15 minutes
500 ml (16 oz)	15 minutes
1 litre (32 oz)	15 minutes

À la casserole

Préparation
40 minutes

Cuisson
20 minutes

Temps de repos
15 minutes

- **sans œuf**
- **sans produits laitiers**
- **sans noix**
- **végé**
- **sans gluten**

6,8 kg (15 lb) de petites betteraves

Pour la marinade:

1,75 litre (7 tasses) d'eau

1,75 litre (7 tasses) de vinaigre blanc à 5 % d'acide acétique

125 ml (½ tasse) de sucre blanc, ou plus au goût (106 g)

15 ml (1 c. à soupe) de grains de coriandre

15 ml (1 c. à soupe) de clous de girofle

15 ml (1 c. à soupe) de gros sel

7,5 ml (½ c. à soupe) de piment de la Jamaïque (quatre-épices) moulu

7,5 ml (½ c. à soupe) de poudre de chili

5 ml (1 c. à thé) de muscade

2 bâtons de cannelle

1. Dans une casserole en acier inoxydable, mélanger tous les ingrédients de la marinade. Porter à ébullition, puis laisser mijoter 5 minutes à feu moyen.

2. Éteindre le feu et laisser infuser la marinade au moins 15 minutes, pendant la préparation des betteraves.

3. Peler les betteraves et les couper en dés ou en tranches de 1 cm (½ po).

4. Déposer les betteraves dans une grande casserole en acier inoxydable et couvrir d'eau. Porter à ébullition, puis cuire de 15 à 20 minutes à feu doux-moyen, jusqu'à ce que les betteraves soient tendres. Égoutter.

5. Répartir les betteraves dans les bocaux, en laissant un espace libre de 1 cm (½ po) entre les betteraves et le rebord des pots.

6. À l'aide d'une passoire fine, filtrer la marinade au-dessus d'une autre casserole en acier inoxydable. Jeter les bâtons de cannelle, les grains de coriandre et les clous de girofle.

7. Porter de nouveau la marinade à ébullition.

8. Verser la marinade bouillante dans les bocaux, en laissant un espace libre de 1 cm (½ po) entre la marinade et le rebord des pots.

9. Plonger un ustensile dans les pots et le remuer afin d'éliminer toute bulle d'air. Au besoin, ajouter de la marinade.

10. Stériliser à la casserole 15 minutes (pour des pots de 250 ml, de 500 ml ou de 1 litre) selon les indications de la page 19.

! Plus il est tôt en saison, plus les betteraves sont petites et tendres, alors que plus la saison avance, plus elles sont grosses et fibreuses. La saveur de la marinade est quant à elle optimale de deux à trois semaines après la mise en conserve. Pour adoucir son goût vinaigré, on peut y ajouter plus de sucre ou remplacer le vinaigre blanc par un vinaigre de cidre à 5 % d'acide acétique. Il est toutefois important de respecter la proportion moitié eau, moitié vinaigre.

Cornichons marinés de Lise

PAR PORTION 1 pot de 1 litre	
Calories	105
Protéines	2 g
M.G.	0 g
Glucides	12 g
Fibres	2 g
Fer	1 mg
Calcium	70 mg
Sodium	3212 mg

STÉRILISATION

QUANTITÉ TOTALE • 5 LITRES (20 TASSES)

Taille des pots	Temps de stérilisation
500 ml (16 oz)	15 minutes
1 litre (32 oz)	15 minutes

À la casserole

Préparation
30 minutes

Trempage
3 heures

Cuisson
10 minutes

- **sans œuf**
- **sans produits laitiers**
- **sans noix**
- **végé**
- **sans gluten**

2,2 litres (2 pintes) de petits cornichons de 7 à 10 cm (de 3 à 4 po) de longueur

5 gousses d'ail (25 g)

5 tiges d'aneth, avec la fleur si possible

2 litres (8 tasses) d'eau

1,5 litre (6 tasses) de vinaigre blanc à 5% d'acide acétique

125 ml (½ tasse) de gros sel (130 g)

1. Laver les cornichons à l'eau froide afin de retirer la terre et les petites épines. Si nécessaire, couper le bout de la tige des cornichons à une longueur de 0,5 cm (¼ de po).

2. Remplir un grand bol d'eau glacée. Déposer les cornichons dans l'eau, en s'assurant qu'ils sont tous bien immergés. Faire tremper les cornichons dans l'eau 3 heures.

3. Placer les cornichons dans les pots à la verticale, en les tassant. Ajouter 1 gousse d'ail et 1 tige d'aneth dans chaque pot (de 500 ml ou de 1 litre), en laissant un espace libre de 1 cm (½ po) entre les aliments et le rebord des pots.

4. Dans une casserole en acier inoxydable, mélanger l'eau avec le vinaigre et le gros sel. Porter à ébullition, puis laisser mijoter 10 minutes à feu moyen, jusqu'à ce que le sel soit complètement dissous.

5. Verser la marinade bouillante dans les bocaux, en laissant un espace libre de 0,5 cm (¼ de po) entre la marinade et le rebord des pots.

6. Plonger un ustensile dans les pots et le remuer afin d'éliminer toute bulle d'air. Au besoin, ajouter de la marinade.

7. Stériliser à la casserole 15 minutes (pour des pots de 500 ml ou de 1 litre) selon les indications de la page 19.

!

Après des années de recherches pour trouver la parfaite recette de cornichons, ma bonne amie Lise Corriveau m'a offert un pot des siens, et ce fut le coup de foudre instantané!

On trouve les petits cornichons seulement tôt en saison, soit vers la fin juillet ou au début août. Il est préférable d'attendre trois semaines après la mise en conserve avant de manger les cornichons, pour laisser le temps aux saveurs de se répandre.

Jardinière de légumes marinés

PAR PORTION 1 pot de 500 ml	
Calories	116
Protéines	4 g
M.G.	1 g
Glucides	19 g
Fibres	6 g
Fer	1 mg
Calcium	80 mg
Sodium	1020 mg

STÉRILISATION

QUANTITÉ TOTALE • 2,5 LITRES (10 TASSES)

Taille des pots	Temps de stérilisation
125 ml (4 oz)	15 minutes
250 ml (8 oz)	15 minutes
500 ml (16 oz)	15 minutes
1 litre (32 oz)	15 minutes

À la casserole

Préparation
40 minutes

Cuisson
5 minutes

Temps de repos
30 minutes

- **sans œuf**
- **sans produits laitiers**
- **sans noix**
- **végé**
- **sans gluten**

500 ml (2 tasses) de chou-fleur coupé en petits bouquets (200 g)

500 ml (2 tasses) de carottes coupées en rondelles de 0,5 cm – ¼ de po (227 g)

500 ml (2 tasses) de courgettes vertes et jaunes coupées en rondelles de 0,5 cm – ¼ de po (239 g)

500 ml (2 tasses) de piments bananes verts et rouges coupés en rondelles de 0,5 cm – ¼ de po (240 g)

500 ml (2 tasses) d'oignons coupés en demi-rondelles de 0,5cm – ¼ de po (240g)

5 feuilles de laurier

Pour la marinade:

750 ml (3 tasses) d'eau

750 ml (3 tasses) de vinaigre blanc à 5 % d'acide acétique

60 ml (¼ de tasse) d'épices à marinades

10 ml (2 c. à thé) de sel, ou plus au goût (facultatif)

6 gousses d'ail (30 g)

1. Dans une casserole en acier inoxydable, mélanger tous les ingrédients de la marinade. Porter à ébullition, puis laisser mijoter 5 minutes à feu moyen.

2. Éteindre le feu et laisser infuser la marinade au moins 30 minutes.

3. À l'aide d'une passoire fine, filtrer la marinade au-dessus d'une autre casserole en acier inoxydable. Jeter l'ail et les épices.

4. Porter de nouveau la marinade à ébullition. Ajouter les légumes et cuire 30 secondes.

5. À l'aide d'une cuillère trouée, répartir les légumes dans les bocaux, en prenant soin de bien les tasser et en laissant un espace libre de 1 cm (½ po) entre les légumes et le rebord des pots.

6. Verser la marinade bouillante dans les bocaux, en laissant un espace libre de 0,5 cm (¼ de po) entre la marinade et le rebord des pots. Ajouter le laurier (¼ de feuille dans chaque pot de 125 ml, ½ feuille dans chaque pot de 250 ml, 1 feuille dans chaque pot de 500 ml et 2 feuilles dans chaque pot de 1 litre).

7. Plonger un ustensile dans les pots et le remuer afin d'éliminer toute bulle d'air. Au besoin, ajouter de la marinade.

8. Stériliser à la casserole 15 minutes (pour des pots de 125 ml, de 250 ml, de 500 ml ou de 1 litre) selon les indications de la page 19.

! *J'aime utiliser un couteau à lame dentelée pour donner un petit look rétro à cette jardinière! La saveur de la marinade sera optimale de deux à trois semaines après la mise en conserve.*

Pikliz

PAR PORTION 1 pot de 250 ml	
Calories	85
Protéines	3 g
M.G.	1 g
Glucides	22 g
Fibres	4 g
Fer	2 mg
Calcium	71 mg
Sodium	149 mg

STÉRILISATION

QUANTITÉ TOTALE • 750 ML (3 TASSES)

Taille des pots	Temps de stérilisation
125 ml (4 oz)	10 minutes
250 ml (8 oz)	10 minutes
500 ml (16 oz)	10 minutes
1 litre (32 oz)	10 minutes

À la casserole

Préparation
10 minutes

Cuisson
5 minutes

Temps de repos
20 minutes

- **sans œuf**
- **sans produits laitiers**
- **sans noix**
- **végé**
- **sans gluten**

500 ml (2 tasses) de chou vert émincé (190 g)

125 ml (½ tasse) de carottes coupées en julienne (45 g)

¼ de poivron rouge émincé (45 g)

¼ de poivron vert émincé (45 g)

60 ml (¼ de tasse) d'oignon émincé (45 g)

1 oignon vert émincé (15 g)

3 piments thaïs (15 g) coupés en rondelles (au goût, facultatif)

1 lime coupée en fines tranches

Pour la marinade:

250 ml (1 tasse) de vinaigre blanc à 5 % d'acide acétique

250 ml (1 tasse) de jus de lime en bouteille

2,5 ml (½ c. à thé) de gros sel

3 clous de girofle

1 grosse gousse d'ail (7 g)

1 lime (zeste)

1. Dans une casserole en acier inoxydable, mélanger tous les ingrédients de la marinade. Porter à ébullition, puis laisser mijoter 5 minutes à feu doux.

2. Éteindre le feu et laisser infuser la marinade 20 minutes.

3. Dans un bol, déposer le chou, les carottes, les poivrons, l'oignon, l'oignon vert et, si désiré, les piments thaïs. Remuer.

4. Répartir les légumes dans les pots en les compactant.

5. Insérer un couteau à l'intérieur des pots, contre la paroi afin de créer une ouverture, et y insérer une tranche de lime

6. À l'aide d'une passoire fine, filtrer la marinade au-dessus d'une autre casserole en acier inoxydable. Jeter l'ail, les clous de girofle et le zeste.

7. Porter de nouveau la marinade à ébullition.

8. Verser la marinade bouillante dans les bocaux, en laissant un espace libre de 0,25 cm (⅛ de po) entre la marinade et le rebord des pots.

9. Plonger un ustensile dans les pots et le remuer afin d'éliminer toute bulle d'air. Au besoin, ajouter de la marinade.

10. Stériliser à la casserole 10 minutes (pour des pots de 125 ml, de 250 ml, de 500 ml ou de 1 litre) selon les indications de la page 19.

!

J'ai découvert le pikliz en voyage et je suis tombée en amour avec le goût unique et la polyvalence de ce condiment haïtien. Il en existe autant de variantes qu'il y a de cuisinières haïtiennes! Bien que la recette classique soit normalement très épicée, on peut ajuster l'intensité selon les goûts de chacun. On le sert comme accompagnement, comme condiment ou comme garniture dans les sandwichs et les burgers, par exemple.

Piments forts marinés

PAR PORTION 1 pot de 125 ml	
Calories	16
Protéines	1 g
M.G.	0 g
Glucides	3 g
Fibres	2 g
Fer	0 mg
Calcium	9 mg
Sodium	6 mg

STÉRILISATION

QUANTITÉ TOTALE • 500 ML (2 TASSES)

Taille des pots	Temps de stérilisation
125 ml (4 oz)	10 minutes
250 ml (8 oz)	10 minutes
500 ml (16 oz)	10 minutes
1 litre (32 oz)	10 minutes

À la casserole

Préparation
10 minutes

Cuisson
6 minutes

- **sans œuf**
- **sans produits laitiers**
- **sans noix**
- **végé**
- **sans gluten**

4 piments bananes (340 g)

60 ml (¼ de tasse) d'eau

60 ml (¼ de tasse) de vinaigre blanc à 5 % d'acide acétique

1 gousse d'ail (5 g)

Sel au goût

Portez des gants pour préparer les piments !

1. Retirer la queue des piments. Si désiré, retirer la membrane blanche et les graines des piments (ce sont la membrane et les graines qui renferment le goût plus piquant des piments : plus vous en conserverez, plus le goût sera intense). Couper les piments en fines rondelles.

2. Dans une casserole en acier inoxydable, mélanger l'eau avec le vinaigre et l'ail. Saler. Porter à ébullition, puis laisser mijoter 5 minutes à feu doux.

3. À l'aide d'une cuillère trouée, retirer l'ail. Ajouter les piments dans la casserole et laisser mijoter 1 minute.

4. Répartir les piments et la marinade dans les bocaux, en laissant un espace libre de 0,5 cm (¼ de po) entre la marinade et le rebord des pots.

5. Plonger un ustensile dans les pots et le remuer afin d'éliminer toute bulle d'air. Au besoin, ajouter de la marinade.

6. Stériliser à la casserole 10 minutes (pour des pots de 125 ml, de 250 ml, de 500 ml ou de 1 litre) selon les indications de la page 19.

! J'utilise le robot culinaire pour trancher rapidement les piments, ou j'utilise un couteau à lame dentelée pour faire différent et joli. Je mets ces piments marinés sur les pizzas, dans les burgers, les tacos et les sandwichs.

PAR PORTION 1 pot de 125 ml	
Calories	58
Protéines	2 g
M.G.	0 g
Glucides	11 g
Fibres	2 g
Fer	1 mg
Calcium	12 mg
Sodium	7 mg

Poivrons doux marinés

STÉRILISATION

QUANTITÉ TOTALE • 500 ML (2 TASSES)

Taille des pots	Temps de stérilisation
125 ml (4 oz)	10 minutes
250 ml (8 oz)	10 minutes
500 ml (16 oz)	10 minutes
1 litre (32 oz)	10 minutes

À la casserole

Préparation
10 minutes

Cuisson
2 minutes

- **sans œuf**
- **sans produits laitiers**
- **sans noix**
- **végé**
- **sans gluten**

4 poivrons rouges, oranges et/ou jaunes (744 g)

60 ml (¼ de tasse) d'eau

60 ml (¼ de tasse) de vinaigre blanc à 5 % d'acide acétique

5 ml (1 c. à thé) de sucre (facultatif)

1. Retirer la membrane blanche et les graines des poivrons, puis couper les poivrons en petits dés.

2. Dans une casserole en acier inoxydable, mélanger l'eau avec le vinaigre, les poivrons et, si désiré, le sucre. Porter à ébullition, puis laisser mijoter 2 minutes à feu moyen.

3. Répartir les poivrons et la marinade dans les bocaux, en laissant un espace libre de 0,5 cm (¼ de po) entre la marinade et le rebord des pots.

4. Plonger un ustensile dans les pots et le remuer afin d'éliminer toute bulle d'air. Au besoin, ajouter de la marinade.

5. Stériliser à la casserole 10 minutes (pour des pots de 125 ml, de 250 ml, de 500 ml ou de 1 litre) selon les indications de la page 19.

Je sers ces poivrons comme accompagnement pour les fromages, les charcuteries, les terrines et les pâtés. Je trouve les poivrons suffisamment sucrés naturellement, mais on peut ajouter un peu de sucre à la marinade pour adoucir davantage le goût vinaigré.

Salade de chou

PAR PORTION 1 pot de 500 ml	
Calories	83
Protéines	2 g
M.G.	0 g
Glucides	14 g
Fibres	4 g
Fer	1 mg
Calcium	83 mg
Sodium	59 mg

STÉRILISATION

QUANTITÉ TOTALE • 1 LITRE (4 TASSES)

Taille des pots	Temps de stérilisation
125 ml (4 oz)	10 minutes
250 ml (8 oz)	10 minutes
500 ml (16 oz)	10 minutes
1 litre (32 oz)	10 minutes

À la casserole

Préparation
10 minutes

Cuisson
1 minute

- **sans œuf**
- **sans produits laitiers**
- **sans noix**
- **végé**
- **sans gluten**

1 litre (4 tasses) de chou vert râpé ou émincé (440 g)

180 ml (¾ de tasse) de carottes râpées ou coupées en julienne (60 g)

250 ml (1 tasse) d'eau

125 ml (½ tasse) de vinaigre blanc à 5 % d'acide acétique

125 ml (½ tasse) de jus de citron en bouteille

2,5 ml (½ c. à thé) de poudre d'oignon

2,5 ml (½ c. à thé) de poudre d'ail

1,25 ml (¼ de c. à thé) de sucre (facultatif)

Sel et poivre au goût

1. Répartir le chou et les carottes dans les pots, en prenant soin de bien les tasser.

2. Dans une casserole en acier inoxydable, mélanger le reste des ingrédients. Porter à ébullition, puis laisser mijoter 1 minute à feu moyen.

3. Verser la marinade bouillante dans les bocaux, en laissant un espace libre de 0,25 cm (⅛ de po) entre la marinade et le rebord des pots.

4. Plonger un ustensile dans les pots et le remuer afin d'éliminer toute bulle d'air. Au besoin, ajouter de la marinade.

5. Stériliser à la casserole 10 minutes (pour des pots de 125 ml, de 250 ml, de 500 ml ou de 1 litre) selon les indications de la page 19.

! Avant de servir, égouttez la salade de chou et arrosez-la d'un filet d'huile végétale. Pour une salade de chou crémeuse, il suffit d'ajouter un peu de mayonnaise, et le tour est joué!

PAR PORTION 1 pot de 500 ml	
Calories	59
Protéines	2 g
M.G.	0 g
Glucides	12 g
Fibres	4 g
Fer	0 mg
Calcium	59 mg
Sodium	78 mg

Légumes nature

STÉRILISATION

QUANTITÉ TOTALE • 3 LITRES (12 TASSES)

Taille des pots	Temps de stérilisation
125 ml (4 oz)	10 minutes
250 ml (8 oz)	10 minutes
500 ml (16 oz)	10 minutes
1 litre (32 oz)	10 minutes

À la casserole

Préparation
25 minutes

- **sans œuf**
- **sans produits laitiers**
- **sans noix**
- **végé**
- **sans gluten**

2 litres (8 tasses) d'eau

10 ml (2 c. à thé) d'acide citrique

3 litres (12 tasses) de légumes au choix parmi les suivants (1 kg – environ 2 ¼ lb) :

Brocolis coupés en petits bouquets

Choux-fleurs coupés en petits bouquets

Carottes coupées en dés ou en rondelles de maximum 2,5 cm (1 po)

Haricots verts ou jaunes coupés en tronçons de 5 cm (2 po)

Poivrons de couleurs variées coupés en dés de 2,5 cm (1 po)

Céleri coupé en tronçons de 2,5 cm (1 po)

Oignons verts coupés en tronçons de 5 cm (2 po)

Pois sucrés coupés en deux sur la longueur

1. Dans une grande casserole en acier inoxydable, mélanger l'eau avec l'acide citrique. Porter à ébullition. Ajouter les légumes et laisser mijoter 30 secondes.

2. À l'aide d'une cuillère trouée, répartir les légumes dans les bocaux, en laissant un espace libre de 1 cm (½ po) entre les légumes et le rebord des pots.

3. Verser l'eau dans les bocaux, en laissant un espace libre de 0,5 cm (¼ de po) entre l'eau et le rebord des pots.

4. Plonger un ustensile dans les pots et le remuer afin d'éliminer toute bulle d'air. Au besoin, ajouter de l'eau.

5. Stériliser à la casserole 10 minutes (pour des pots de 125 ml, de 250 ml, de 500 ml ou de 1 litre) selon les indications de la page 19.

! L'ajout de l'acide citrique est capital dans cette recette : il permet de stériliser les pots à la casserole plutôt qu'à l'autoclave, en plus de garder les légumes les plus croquants possible et de préserver un maximum de leurs vitamines. Soyez sans crainte, l'acide citrique ne changera pas le goût des légumes.

SOUPES

La soupe est sans doute le plat le plus réconfortant de l'univers ! Quoi de mieux qu'une bonne soupe chaude maison quand on est malade, qu'on a le cœur gros ou simplement quand il fait froid dehors ? Les soupes sont les premières conserves du commerce qui ont disparu de chez moi le jour où j'ai reçu mon premier autoclave. Découvrez ici des recettes de soupes classiques, mais aussi des recettes qui vous feront voyager !

Soupe rapide poulet et nouilles

PAR PORTION 500 ml (2 tasses) de soupe préparée	
Calories	155
Protéines	17 g
M.G.	4 g
Glucides	12 g
Fibres	2 g
Fer	1 mg
Calcium	41 mg
Sodium	936 mg

STÉRILISATION

QUANTITÉ TOTALE • 1,5 LITRE (6 TASSES)

Taille des pots	Temps de stérilisation
500 ml (16 oz)	60 minutes
1 litre (32 oz)	75 minutes

Préparation
5 minutes

Cuisson
5 minutes

- **sans œuf**
- **sans produits laitiers**
- **sans noix**

750 ml (3 tasses) de bouillon de dinde (voir recette à la page 40)

250 ml (1 tasse) de poulet cuit coupé en dés (180 g)

125 ml (½ tasse) d'oignon coupé en dés (70 g)

125 ml (½ tasse) de céleri coupé en dés (70 g)

125 ml (½ tasse) de carotte coupée en dés (70 g)

90 à 125 ml (6 c. à soupe à ½ tasse) de nouilles à soupe au choix

1. Dans une casserole en acier inoxydable, porter le bouillon de dinde à ébullition.

2. Répartir le poulet cuit, l'oignon, le céleri et la carotte dans les pots.

3. Verser le bouillon bouillant dans les bocaux, en laissant un espace libre de 2,5 cm (1 po) entre le bouillon et le rebord des pots.

4. Plonger un ustensile dans les pots et le remuer afin d'éliminer toute bulle d'air. Au besoin, ajouter du bouillon.

5. Stériliser à l'autoclave (60 minutes pour des pots de 500 ml et 75 minutes pour des pots de 1 litre) selon les indications de la page 20.

6. Au moment de servir, porter la soupe à ébullition à feu moyen dans une casserole. Ajouter 30 ml (2 c. à soupe) de nouilles pour chaque pot de 500 ml et 60 ml (¼ de tasse) de nouilles pour chaque pot de 1 litre. Cuire les nouilles dans la soupe selon les indications de l'emballage.

PAR PORTION 1 pot de 500 ml	
Calories	129
Protéines	4 g
M.G.	4 g
Glucides	19 g
Fibres	5 g
Fer	2 mg
Calcium	84 mg
Sodium	1092 mg

Soupe tomates et orge

STÉRILISATION

QUANTITÉ TOTALE • 4 LITRES (8 TASSES)

Taille des pots	Temps de stérilisation
500 ml (16 oz)	60 minutes
1 litre (32 oz)	75 minutes

À l'autoclave

Préparation
10 minutes

Cuisson
13 minutes

- sans œuf
- sans produits laitiers
- sans noix

30 ml (2 c. à soupe) d'huile végétale

250 ml (1 tasse) d'oignon haché (140 g)

750 ml (3 tasses) de carottes coupées en dés (420 g)

125 ml (½ tasse) de céleri coupé en dés (70 g)

2 gousses d'ail hachées (10 g)

2 litres (8 tasses) de bouillon de dinde (voir recette à la page 40)

1 litre (4 tasses) de tomates coupées en dés

15 ml (1 c. à soupe) de persil séché

Sel et poivre au goût

120 ml (8 c. à soupe) d'orge mondé (110 g)

1. Dans une grande casserole en acier inoxydable, chauffer l'huile à feu moyen. Cuire l'oignon, les carottes et le céleri 7 minutes.

2. Ajouter l'ail et poursuivre la cuisson 1 minute.

3. Ajouter le bouillon, les tomates et le persil. Saler et poivrer. Porter à ébullition, puis laisser mijoter 5 minutes à feu moyen.

4. Déposer 15 ml (1 c. à soupe) d'orge mondé dans chacun des pots de 500 ml et 30 ml (2 c. à soupe) d'orge mondé dans chacun des pots de 1 litre.

5. À l'aide d'une cuillère trouée, répartir les aliments solides dans les pots.

6. Verser le bouillon bouillant dans les bocaux, en laissant un espace libre de 2,5 cm (1 po) entre le bouillon et le rebord des pots.

7. Plonger un ustensile dans les pots et le remuer afin d'éliminer toute bulle d'air. Au besoin, ajouter du bouillon.

8. Stériliser à l'autoclave (60 minutes pour des pots de 500 ml et 75 minutes pour des pots de 1 litre) selon les indications de la page 20.

! Cette recette simple et délicieuse provient de ma belle-mère Diane Lafleur (merci Diane!).

Velouté de courge poivrée

PAR PORTION 1 pot de 500 ml	
Calories	196
Protéines	4 g
M.G.	4 g
Glucides	41 g
Fibres	7 g
Fer	2 mg
Calcium	108 mg
Sodium	897 mg

STÉRILISATION

QUANTITÉ TOTALE • 4 LITRES (16 TASSES)

Taille des pots	Temps de stérilisation
500 ml (16 oz)	35 minutes
1 litre (32 oz)	45 minutes

À l'autoclave

Préparation
30 minutes

Cuisson
40 minutes

- sans œuf
- sans produits laitiers
- sans noix

1 courge poivrée de 1,8 kg (4 lb)

30 ml (2 c. à soupe) d'huile végétale

250 ml (1 tasse) d'oignon haché (140 g)

500 ml (2 tasses) de carottes coupées en dés (280 g)

750 ml (3 tasses) de pommes coupées en dés (600 g)

2 gousses d'ail hachées (10 g)

2 litres (8 tasses) de bouillon au choix (voir recettes aux pages 30, 32 et 40)

Sel et poivre au goût

1. Préchauffer le four à 205 °C (400 °F).

2. Couper la courge en deux sur la longueur. Retirer les graines et les filaments.

3. Sur une plaque de cuisson tapissée de papier parchemin, déposer les demi-courges, côté chair vers le bas.

4. Cuire au four 40 minutes, jusqu'à ce que la pointe d'un couteau transperce facilement la chair de la courge. Retirer du four et laisser tiédir avant de retirer la chair de la courge à l'aide d'une cuillère. Réserver.

5. Pendant ce temps, chauffer l'huile à feu moyen dans une grande casserole en acier inoxydable. Cuire l'oignon 7 minutes.

6. Ajouter les carottes et les pommes. Poursuivre la cuisson 7 minutes en remuant de temps en temps.

7. Ajouter l'ail et cuire 1 minute en remuant.

8. Ajouter le bouillon et la chair de la courge dans la casserole. Saler et poivrer. Porter à ébullition, puis laisser mijoter 5 minutes à feu moyen. Goûter et rectifier l'assaisonnement au besoin.

9. À l'aide d'une cuillère trouée, répartir les aliments solides dans les pots.

10. Verser le bouillon bouillant dans les bocaux, en laissant un espace libre de 2,5 cm (1 po) entre le bouillon et le rebord des pots.

11. Plonger un ustensile dans les pots et le remuer afin d'éliminer toute bulle d'air. Au besoin, ajouter du bouillon.

12. Stériliser à l'autoclave (35 minutes pour des pots de 500 ml et 45 minutes pour des pots de 1 litre) selon les indications de la page 20.

13. Au moment de servir, verser la préparation dans le contenant du mélangeur électrique. Mélanger la préparation jusqu'à l'obtention d'une purée lisse. Verser le velouté dans une casserole et réchauffer quelques minutes à feu moyen. Ajouter un peu de crème ou de beurre pour un goût plus riche et velouté.

PAR PORTION 1 pot de 500 ml	
Calories	330
Protéines	7 g
M.G.	10 g
Glucides	41 g
Fibres	5 g
Fer	2 mg
Calcium	77 mg
Sodium	1170 mg

Soupe antillaise

STÉRILISATION

QUANTITÉ TOTALE • 1,5 LITRE (6 TASSES)

À l'autoclave

Taille des pots	Temps de stérilisation
500 ml (16 oz)	35 minutes
1 litre (32 oz)	45 minutes

Préparation
20 minutes

Cuisson
14 minutes

- **sans œuf**
- **sans produits laitiers**
- **sans noix**
- **sans gluten**

500 ml (2 tasses) de pommes de terre Russet pelées et coupées en dés de 1 cm – ½ po (400 g)

15 ml (1 c. à soupe) d'huile végétale

500 ml (2 tasses) d'oignons coupés en dés (280 g)

2 gousses d'ail hachées (10 g)

1 petit piment thaï haché finement, ou plus au goût (5 g)

250 ml (1 tasse) de vin blanc sec

1 litre (4 tasses) de bouillon au choix (voir recettes aux pages 30, 32 et 40)

80 ml (⅓ de tasse) de ciboulette fraîche hachée (30 g)

Sel et poivre au goût

1. Rincer les dés de pommes de terre à l'eau froide, puis les répartir dans les pots.

2. Dans une grande casserole en acier inoxydable, chauffer l'huile à feu moyen. Cuire les oignons 7 minutes.

3. Ajouter l'ail et le piment thaï. Poursuivre la cuisson 2 minutes.

4. Déglacer avec le vin blanc en raclant le fond de la casserole avec une cuillère en bois afin de détacher les sucs de cuisson. Ajouter le bouillon et la ciboulette. Saler et poivrer. Porter à ébullition, puis laisser mijoter 5 minutes à feu doux.

5. À l'aide d'une cuillère trouée, répartir les aliments solides dans les pots.

6. Verser le bouillon bouillant dans les bocaux, en laissant un espace libre de 2,5 cm (1 po) entre le liquide et le rebord des pots.

7. Plonger un ustensile dans les pots et le remuer afin d'éliminer toute bulle d'air. Au besoin, ajouter du bouillon.

8. Stériliser à l'autoclave (35 minutes pour des pots de 500 ml et 45 minutes pour des pots de 1 litre) selon les indications de la page 20.

! On trouve des variantes de cette recette un peu partout dans les Antilles, les Caraïbes et au Mexique sous différents noms (soupe à l'oignon, soupe à la pomme de terre, soupe à l'igname Pakala, etc.). On la sert en entrée pour se réchauffer, mais elle peut aussi être servie comme plat principal, puisqu'elle est bien consistante. J'aime y ajouter une protéine au moment de servir pour en faire un repas complet.

Soupe asiatique aux edamames

PAR PORTION 1 pot de 500 ml	
Calories	237
Protéines	17 g
M.G.	12 g
Glucides	19 g
Fibres	7 g
Fer	4 mg
Calcium	114 mg
Sodium	2388 mg

STÉRILISATION

QUANTITÉ TOTALE • 1,5 LITRE (6 TASSES)

Taille des pots	Temps de stérilisation
500 ml (16 oz)	40 minutes
1 litre (32 oz)	50 minutes

À l'autoclave

Préparation
15 minutes

Cuisson
7 minutes

- sans œuf
- sans produits laitiers
- sans gluten

500 ml (2 tasses) d'edamames décortiqués surgelés (275 g)

15 ml (1 c. à soupe) d'huile de sésame (non grillé)

2 gousses d'ail hachées (10 g)

15 ml (1 c. à soupe) de gingembre haché (11 g)

1 petit piment thaï haché (5 g)

45 ml (3 c. à soupe) de miso (52 g)

1,5 litre (6 tasses) de bouillon au choix (voir recettes aux pages 30, 32 et 40)

250 ml (1 tasse) d'épinards (32 g)

Sel et poivre au goût

1. Répartir les edamames dans les pots.

2. Dans une casserole en acier inoxydable, chauffer l'huile à feu moyen. Cuire l'ail, le gingembre et le piment thaï 2 minutes.

3. Ajouter le miso, le bouillon et les épinards. Saler et poivrer. Porter à ébullition, puis laisser mijoter 5 minutes à feu doux-moyen. Goûter et rectifier l'assaisonnement au besoin.

4. À l'aide d'une cuillère trouée, répartir les aliments solides dans les pots.

5. Verser le bouillon bouillant dans les bocaux, en laissant un espace libre de 2,5 cm (1 po) entre le bouillon et le rebord des pots.

6. Plonger un ustensile dans les pots et le remuer afin d'éliminer toute bulle d'air. Au besoin, ajouter du bouillon.

7. Stériliser à l'autoclave (40 minutes pour des pots de 500 ml et 50 minutes pour des pots de 1 litre) selon les indications de la page 20.

! Au moment de réchauffer la soupe, j'aime y ajouter des nouilles instantanées de style ramen pour la rendre plus consistante! Ensuite, je la garnis toujours de coriandre fraîche et d'oignons verts.

Soupe-repas cajun aux gombos

PAR PORTION 1 pot de 500 ml	
Calories	397
Protéines	31 g
M.G.	25 g
Glucides	13 g
Fibres	4 g
Fer	3 mg
Calcium	116 mg
Sodium	1738 mg

STÉRILISATION

QUANTITÉ TOTALE • 3 LITRES (12 TASSES)

Taille des pots	Temps de stérilisation
250 ml (8 oz)	65 minutes
500 ml (16 oz)	75 minutes
1 litre (32 oz)	90 minutes

À l'autoclave

Préparation
30 minutes

Cuisson
19 minutes

- **sans œuf**
- **sans produits laitiers**
- **sans noix**

4 saucisses italiennes (ou autre saveur au choix) coupées en tranches de 1 cm – ½ po

500 ml (2 tasses) de dinde (375 g) cuite (voir recette à la page 40)

45 ml (3 c. à soupe) d'huile végétale

250 ml (1 tasse) d'oignon coupé en dés (140 g)

500 ml (2 tasses) de céleri coupé en dés (280 g)

250 ml (1 tasse) de poivron vert coupé en dés (200 g)

625 ml (2 ½ tasses) de gombos (okras) coupés en rondelles de 1 cm – ½ po (350 g)

3 gousses d'ail hachées (15 g)

30 ml (2 c. à soupe) de mélange d'épices cajun (voir recette à la page 44)

2 litres (8 tasses) de bouillon de dinde ou de fumet de poisson et fruits de mer (voir recettes aux pages 40 et 34)

2 feuilles de laurier émiettées

60 ml (¼ tasse) de persil frais haché (7 g)

Sauce piquante (facultatif, au goût)

Sel et poivre au goût

1. Chauffer une grande casserole en acier inoxydable à feu moyen. Cuire les saucisses de 4 à 5 minutes. Ajouter la dinde et poursuivre la cuisson 2 minutes, jusqu'à ce qu'elle soit dorée.

2. Répartir les saucisses et la dinde dans les pots.

3. Dans la même casserole, chauffer l'huile à feu moyen-élevé. Cuire l'oignon, le céleri, le poivron et les gombos 7 minutes.

4. Ajouter l'ail et les épices cajun. Poursuivre la cuisson 1 minute.

5. Déglacer avec le bouillon en raclant le fond de la casserole avec une cuillère en bois afin de détacher les sucs de cuisson. Ajouter les feuilles de laurier, le persil et, si désiré, la sauce piquante. Saler, poivrer et remuer. Laisser mijoter 5 minutes. Goûter et rectifier l'assaisonnement au besoin.

6. À l'aide d'une cuillère trouée, répartir les aliments solides dans les pots.

7. Verser le bouillon bouillant dans les bocaux, en laissant un espace libre de 2,5 cm (1 po) entre le bouillon et le rebord des pots.

8. Plonger un ustensile dans les pots et le remuer afin d'éliminer toute bulle d'air. Au besoin, ajouter du bouillon.

9. Stériliser à l'autoclave (65 minutes pour des pots de 250 ml, 75 minutes pour des pots de 500 ml et 90 minutes pour des pots de 1 litre) selon les indications de la page 20.

10. Au moment de servir, verser le contenu d'un pot dans une casserole. Délayer de la fécule de maïs (7,5 ml – ½ c. à soupe pour un pot de 250 ml, 15 ml – 1 c. à soupe pour un pot de 500 ml ou 30 ml – 2 c. à soupe pour un pot de 1 litre) dans un peu d'eau froide, puis l'incorporer à la soupe. Réchauffer quelques minutes.

! Le gombo traditionnel cajun est un plat très réconfortant, mais il faut souvent toute une journée pour le cuisiner. Cette soupe très consistante, qui rappelle presque le ragoût, offre un beau raccourci de temps lorsqu'on la met en conserve, puisqu'il suffit de la réchauffer au moment de servir. On trouve les gombos, aussi appelés « okras », frais dans certaines épiceries, mais plus souvent surgelés en sac: ceux-ci conviendront très bien à cette recette.

PAR PORTION 1 pot de 500 ml	
Calories	222
Protéines	5 g
M.G.	9 g
Glucides	28 g
Fibres	5 g
Fer	1 mg
Calcium	89 mg
Sodium	1421 mg

Soupe à l'oignon

STÉRILISATION

QUANTITÉ TOTALE • 2,5 LITRES (10 TASSES)

Taille des pots	Temps de stérilisation
500 ml (16 oz)	35 minutes
1 litre (32 oz)	45 minutes

À l'autoclave

Préparation
20 minutes

Cuisson
35 minutes

- sans œuf
- sans produits laitiers
- sans noix
- sans gluten

45 ml (3 c. à soupe) d'huile végétale

3 litres (12 tasses) d'oignons coupés en demi-rondelles (1,6 kg)

1 gousse d'ail hachée (5 g)

1 pincée de sel

125 ml (½ tasse) de vin blanc sec

2 litres (8 tasses) de bouillon au choix (voir recettes aux pages 30, 32 et 40)

5 ml (1 c. à thé) de thym séché

Poivre au goût

1. Dans une grande casserole en acier inoxydable, chauffer l'huile à feu doux-moyen. Cuire les oignons, l'ail et le sel 30 minutes en remuant de temps en temps, jusqu'à ce que les oignons soient caramélisés.

2. Déglacer avec le vin en raclant le fond de la casserole avec une cuillère en bois afin de détacher les sucs de cuisson. Ajouter le bouillon et le thym. Poivrer. Porter à ébullition, puis laisser mijoter 5 minutes à feu doux.

3. À l'aide d'une cuillère trouée, répartir les aliments solides dans les pots.

4. Verser le bouillon bouillant dans les bocaux, en laissant un espace libre de 2,5 cm (1 po) entre le bouillon et le rebord des pots.

5. Plonger un ustensile dans les pots et le remuer afin d'éliminer toute bulle d'air. Au besoin, ajouter du bouillon.

6. Stériliser à l'autoclave (35 minutes pour des pots de 500 ml et 45 minutes pour des pots de 1 litre) selon les indications de la page 20.

! *J'aime bien servir cette recette telle quelle, mais on peut évidemment l'agrémenter de croûtons gratinés au four pour en faire une version classique.*

Soupe thaïe crémeuse au poulet

PAR PORTION 1 pot de 500 ml	
Calories	344
Protéines	38 g
M.G.	14 g
Glucides	16 g
Fibres	4 g
Fer	2 mg
Calcium	73 mg
Sodium	1284 mg

STÉRILISATION

QUANTITÉ TOTALE • 1,5 LITRE (6 TASSES)

Taille des pots	Temps de stérilisation
500 ml (16 oz)	60 minutes
1 litre (32 oz)	75 minutes

À l'autoclave

Préparation
25 minutes

Cuisson
19 minutes

- sans œuf
- sans produits laitiers

250 ml (1 tasse) de haricots verts coupés en tronçons de 2,5 cm (1 po), frais ou surgelés (125 g)

180 ml (¾ de tasse) de carotte coupée en dés (100 g)

15 ml (1 c. à soupe) d'huile de sésame (non grillé)

450 g (1 lb) de poitrine de poulet désossée sans peau coupée en dés de 2,5 cm (1 po)

250 ml (1 tasse) d'oignon coupé en dés (140 g)

2 gousses d'ail hachées (10 g)

15 ml (1 c. à soupe) de gingembre haché

1 piment thaï émincé, facultatif (5 g)

1 litre (4 tasses) de bouillon de dinde (voir recette à la page 40)

5 ml (1 c. à thé) de pâte de cari rouge

5 ml (1 c. à thé) de curcuma

Sel et poivre au goût

1. Répartir les haricots verts et la carotte dans les pots.

2. Dans une casserole en acier inoxydable, chauffer la moitié de l'huile de sésame à feu moyen. Cuire les dés de poulet de 5 à 7 minutes, jusqu'à ce que l'intérieur de la chair du poulet ait perdu sa teinte rosée.

3. Répartir le poulet cuit dans les pots.

4. Dans la même casserole, chauffer le reste de l'huile à feu moyen. Cuire l'oignon 7 minutes.

5. Ajouter l'ail, le gingembre et, si désiré, le piment thaï dans la casserole. Poursuivre la cuisson 2 minutes.

6. Déglacer avec le bouillon en raclant le fond de la casserole avec une cuillère en bois afin de détacher les sucs de cuisson. Ajouter la pâte de cari rouge et le curcuma. Saler et poivrer. Porter à ébullition, puis laisser mijoter 5 minutes à feu doux-moyen.

7. À l'aide d'une cuillère trouée, répartir les aliments solides dans les pots.

8. Verser le bouillon bouillant dans les bocaux, en laissant un espace libre de 2,5 cm (1 po) entre le bouillon et le rebord des pots.

9. Plonger un ustensile dans les pots et le remuer afin d'éliminer toute bulle d'air. Au besoin, ajouter du bouillon.

10. Stériliser à l'autoclave (60 minutes pour des pots de 500 ml et 75 minutes pour des pots de 1 litre) selon les indications de la page 20.

Au moment de réchauffer la soupe, ajoutez un peu de lait de coco à la préparation. Garnissez ensuite chaque portion de coriandre fraîche et d'oignons verts hachés.

PAR PORTION 1 pot de 500 ml	
Calories	627
Protéines	51 g
M.G.	37 g
Glucides	20 g
Fibres	4 g
Fer	5 mg
Calcium	71 mg
Sodium	1261 mg

Noces à l'italienne

STÉRILISATION

QUANTITÉ TOTALE • 2 LITRES (8 TASSES)

Taille des pots	Temps de stérilisation
500 ml (16 oz)	75 minutes
1 litre (32 oz)	90 minutes

À l'autoclave

Préparation
20 minutes

Cuisson
10 minutes

- **sans produits laitiers**
- **sans noix**

900 g (2 lb) de porc haché maigre

250 ml (1 tasse) d'oignon haché très finement (140 g)

2 gousses d'ail hachées (10 g)

1 œuf battu

60 ml (¼ de tasse) de chapelure nature

5 ml (1 c. à thé) de romarin séché

Sel et poivre au goût

1,25 litre (5 tasses) de bouillon de bœuf (voir recette à la page 30)

15 ml (1 c. à soupe) de persil frais haché

1 contenant de bébés épinards de 142 g grossièrement hachés

60 ml (¼ de tasse) d'orge mondé

1. Préchauffer le four à 260 °C (500 °F).

2. Dans un bol, mélanger le porc avec l'oignon, l'ail, l'œuf, la chapelure et le romarin. Saler et poivrer.

3. Façonner des boulettes de 2,5 cm (1 po) de diamètre en utilisant 15 ml (1 c. à soupe) de préparation pour chacune d'elles.

4. Déposer les boulettes sur une plaque de cuisson tapissée de papier parchemin. Cuire au four 10 minutes.

5. Pendant ce temps, porter le bouillon de bœuf à ébullition dans une casserole en acier inoxydable. Ajouter le persil et les bébés épinards. Laisser mijoter 5 minutes à feu doux.

6. Déposer 15 ml (1 c. à soupe) d'orge mondé dans chaque pot de 500 ml ou 30 ml (2 c. à soupe) dans chaque pot de 1 litre.

7. Répartir les boulettes cuites dans les pots de manière à remplir la moitié de chaque pot.

8. Verser le bouillon bouillant dans les bocaux, en laissant un espace libre de 2,5 cm (1 po) entre le bouillon et le rebord des pots.

9. Plonger un ustensile dans les pots et le remuer afin d'éliminer toute bulle d'air. Au besoin, ajouter du bouillon.

10. Stériliser à l'autoclave (75 minutes pour des pots de 500 ml et 90 minutes pour des pots de 1 litre) selon les indications de la page 20.

Soupe minestrone de ma mère

PAR PORTION 1 pot de 500 ml	
Calories	140
Protéines	6 g
M.G.	2 g
Glucides	25 g
Fibres	6 g
Fer	3 mg
Calcium	123 mg
Sodium	812 mg

STÉRILISATION

QUANTITÉ TOTALE • 4 LITRES (16 TASSES)

Taille des pots	Temps de stérilisation
500 ml (16 oz)	60 minutes
1 litre (32 oz)	75 minutes

À l'autoclave

Préparation
15 minutes

Trempage
12 heures

Cuisson
11 minutes

- **sans œuf**
- **sans produits laitiers**
- **sans noix**
- **sans gluten**

160 ml (⅔ de tasse) de haricots blancs secs (170 g)

15 ml (1 c. à soupe) d'huile végétale

500 ml (2 tasses) d'oignons coupés en dés (280 g)

375 ml (1 ½ tasse) de céleri coupé en dés (210 g)

500 ml (2 tasses) de carottes coupées en dés (280 g)

125 ml (½ tasse) d'épinards grossièrement hachés (16 g)

3 gousses d'ail hachées (15 g)

2 litres (8 tasses) de bouillon au choix (voir recettes aux pages 30, 32 et 40)

1 boîte de tomates en dés de 796 ml

5 ml (1 c. à thé) de basilic séché

5 ml (1 c. à thé) d'origan séché

Sel et poivre au goût

1. La veille, rincer les haricots à l'eau froide à l'aide d'une passoire fine. Déposer les haricots dans un grand bol. Couvrir d'eau froide et laisser tremper de 12 à 18 heures au frais..

2. Au moment de la cuisson, égoutter les haricots et jeter l'eau de trempage. Rincer les haricots à l'eau froide et égoutter de nouveau.

3. Dans une grande casserole en acier inoxydable, chauffer l'huile à feu moyen. Cuire les oignons, le céleri, les carottes et les épinards de 5 à 7 minutes.

4. Ajouter l'ail et poursuivre la cuisson 1 minute.

5. Ajouter le bouillon, les haricots, les tomates en dés, le basilic et l'origan. Saler et poivrer. Porter à ébullition, puis laisser mijoter 5 minutes à feu moyen. Goûter et rectifier l'assaisonnement au besoin.

6. À l'aide d'une cuillère trouée, répartir les aliments solides dans les pots.

7. Verser le bouillon bouillant dans les bocaux, en laissant un espace libre de 2,5 cm (1 po) entre le bouillon et le rebord des pots.

8. Plonger un ustensile dans les pots et le remuer afin d'éliminer toute bulle d'air. Au besoin, ajouter du bouillon.

9. Stériliser à l'autoclave (60 minutes pour des pots de 500 ml et 75 minutes pour des pots de 1 litre) selon les indications de la page 20.

! Lorsque j'ai demandé à ma mère la recette de sa bonne soupe, elle m'a avoué ne l'avoir jamais notée! Alors voilà maman, c'est maintenant fait et même imprimé pour la postérité!

VOLAILLE

La volaille est incontournable pour la mise en conserve. Elle plaît à tous, et son goût délicat se marie bien à toutes sortes d'épices et de saveurs. Dans cette section, découvrez des recettes comme un chili à la dinde, que vous pourrez déguster seul ou accompagné de croustilles de maïs, une polyvalente préparation de volaille pour garnir vos vol-au-vent, et bien plus !

PAR PORTION 1 pot de 500 ml	
Calories	600
Protéines	47 g
M.G.	35 g
Glucides	24 g
Fibres	3 g
Fer	3 mg
Calcium	67 mg
Sodium	1228 mg

Préparation de volaille

STÉRILISATION

QUANTITÉ TOTALE • 7 LITRES (28 TASSES)

À l'autoclave

Taille des pots	Temps de stérilisation
250 ml (8 oz)	65 minutes
500 ml (16 oz)	75 minutes
1 litre (32 oz)	90 minutes

Préparation
30 minutes

Cuisson
7 minutes

- **sans œuf**
- **sans noix**

3,5 litres (14 tasses) de viande de dinde (2 kg) cuite et coupée en dés (voir recette à la page 40)

580 ml (2 ⅓ tasses) de carottes coupées en dés (325 g)

580 ml (2 ⅓ tasses) de céleri coupé en dés (325 g)

580 ml (2 ⅓ tasses) de pois verts surgelés (278 g)

580 ml (2 ⅓ tasses) de maïs surgelé (325 g)

3,5 litres (14 tasses) de bouillon de poulet ou de dinde (voir recette à la page 40)

15 ml (1 c. à soupe) de persil séché

15 ml (1 c. à soupe) de poudre d'ail

15 ml (1 c. à soupe) de poudre d'oignon

Sel et poivre au goût

210 ml (¾ de tasse + 2 c. à soupe) de beurre

210 ml (¾ de tasse + 2 c. à soupe) de farine

1. Répartir la dinde et les légumes dans les bocaux, en laissant un espace libre de 2,5 cm (1 po) entre les aliments et le rebord des pots.

2. Dans une casserole en acier inoxydable, mélanger le bouillon avec le persil, la poudre d'ail et la poudre d'oignon. Saler et poivrer. Porter à ébullition à feu élevé. Goûter et rectifier l'assaisonnement au besoin.

3. Verser le bouillon bouillant dans les bocaux, en laissant un espace libre de 2,5 cm (1 po) entre le bouillon et le rebord des pots.

4. Plonger un ustensile dans les pots et le remuer afin d'éliminer toute bulle d'air. Au besoin, ajouter du bouillon.

5. Stériliser à l'autoclave (65 minutes pour des pots de 250 ml, 75 minutes pour des pots de 500 ml et 90 minutes pour des pots de 1 litre) selon les indications de la page 20.

6. Au moment de servir, faire fondre le beurre (15 ml – 1 c. à soupe pour un pot de 250 ml ou de 500 ml, ou 30 ml – 2 c. à soupe pour un pot de 1 litre) à feu moyen dans une casserole en acier inoxydable. Ajouter la farine (15 ml – 1 c. à soupe pour un pot de 250 ml ou de 500 ml, ou 30 ml – 2 c. à soupe pour un pot de 1 litre) et cuire 1 minute en remuant.

7. Verser graduellement le bouillon dans la casserole en remuant constamment. Cuire de 3 à 5 minutes, jusqu'à épaississement.

8. Ajouter la viande et les légumes. Poursuivre la cuisson de 3 à 4 minutes.

! Cette recette est très polyvalente. Elle peut servir de garniture pour les pâtés ou les vol-au-vent, mais elle est aussi délicieuse avec des pâtes.

Yassa (poulet sénégalais)

PAR PORTION 1 pot de 500 ml	
Calories	406
Protéines	43 g
M.G.	13 g
Glucides	31 g
Fibres	6 g
Fer	2 mg
Calcium	97 mg
Sodium	850 mg

STÉRILISATION

QUANTITÉ TOTALE • 3 LITRES (12 TASSES)

Taille des pots	Temps de stérilisation
250 ml (8 oz)	65 minutes
500 ml (16 oz)	75 minutes
1 litre (32 oz)	90 minutes

À l'autoclave

Préparation
30 minutes

Cuisson
12 minutes

- **sans œuf**
- **sans produits laitiers**
- **sans noix**

45 ml (3 c. à soupe) de moutarde de Dijon

1 litre (4 tasses) de bouillon de poulet ou de dinde (voir recette à la page 40)

45 ml (3 c. à soupe) d'huile végétale

1 kg (environ 2 ¼ lb) de chair de poulet (poitrines, hauts de cuisses, etc.) cru, désossé et sans peau, coupée en cubes de 2,5 cm (1 po)

6 oignons coupés en demi-rondelles (840 g)

4 gousses d'ail hachées (20 g)

375 ml (1 ½ tasse) de poivron rouge coupé en lanières (210 g)

375 ml (1 ½ tasse) de poivron vert coupé en lanières (210 g)

60 ml (¼ de tasse) de jalapeño (45 g) épépiné et coupé en rondelles (facultatif, au goût)

250 ml (1 tasse) de jus de lime

3 feuilles de laurier émiettées

5 ml (1 c. à thé) de thym frais ou séché

10 ml (2 c. à thé) de grains de coriandre

5 ml (1 c. à thé) de cumin

10 ml (2 c. à thé) de paprika

2,5 ml (½ c. à thé) de cardamome moulue

2,5 ml (½ c. à thé) de sumac (facultatif)

Sel et poivre au goût

1. Dans un bol, fouetter la moutarde avec le bouillon. Réserver.

2. Dans une grande casserole en acier inoxydable, chauffer l'huile à feu moyen-élevé. Faire dorer les cubes de poulet de 2 à 3 minutes.

3. Ajouter les oignons dans la casserole. Poursuivre la cuisson de 2 à 3 minutes.

4. Ajouter l'ail, les poivrons et, si désiré, le jalapeño. Poursuivre la cuisson 3 minutes.

5. Déglacer avec le jus de lime, en raclant le fond de la casserole avec une cuillère en bois afin de détacher les sucs de cuisson.

6. Ajouter le reste des ingrédients dans la casserole. Saler, poivrer et remuer. Porter à ébullition, puis laisser mijoter 5 minutes à feu doux-moyen.

7. À l'aide d'une cuillère trouée, répartir les aliments solides dans les bocaux, en laissant un espace libre de 2,5 cm (1 po) entre les aliments et le rebord des pots.

8. Verser le bouillon bouillant dans les bocaux, en laissant un espace libre de 2,5 cm (1 po) entre le bouillon et le rebord des pots.

9. Plonger un ustensile dans les pots et le remuer afin d'éliminer toute bulle d'air. Au besoin, ajouter du bouillon.

10. Stériliser à l'autoclave (65 minutes pour des pots de 250 ml, 75 minutes pour des pots de 500 ml et 90 minutes pour des pots de 1 litre) selon les indications de la page 20.

PAR PORTION 1 pot de 500 ml	
Calories	463
Protéines	57 g
M.G.	11 g
Glucides	50 g
Fibres	12 g
Fer	8 mg
Calcium	178 mg
Sodium	450 mg

Chili à la dinde

STÉRILISATION

QUANTITÉ TOTALE • 6,5 LITRES (26 TASSES)

À l'autoclave

Taille des pots	Temps de stérilisation
250 ml (8 oz)	65 minutes
500 ml (16 oz)	75 minutes
1 litre (32 oz)	90 minutes

Préparation
45 minutes

Trempage
12 heures

Cuisson
15 minutes

- sans œuf
- sans produits laitiers
- sans noix
- sans gluten

625 ml (2 ½ tasses) de haricots blancs secs (450 g)

30 ml (2 c. à soupe) d'huile végétale

750 ml (3 tasses) d'oignons hachés (420 g)

6 gousses d'ail hachées (30 g)

500 ml (2 tasses) de céleri haché (280 g)

500 ml (2 tasses) de carottes hachées (280 g)

500 ml (2 tasses) de poivrons de couleurs variées hachés (400 g)

250 ml (1 tasse) de piments bananes épépinés et hachés (200 g)

1,8 kg (4 lb) de viande de dinde cuite et coupée en petits dés (voir recette à la page 40)

500 ml (2 tasses) de maïs frais ou surgelé (300 g)

3 litres (12 tasses) de coulis de tomates (voir recette à la page 28)

500 ml (2 tasses) de bouillon de dinde (voir recette à la page 40)

30 ml (2 c. à soupe) de mélange d'épices mexicain (voir recette à la page 44)

30 ml (2 c. à soupe) de sauce piquante (facultatif, au goût)

1. La veille, faire tremper les haricots dans 1,5 litre (6 tasses) d'eau froide de 12 à 18 heures au frais. Le lendemain, égoutter les haricots et jeter l'eau de trempage. Rincer les haricots à l'eau froide et égoutter de nouveau. Réserver.

2. Dans une grande casserole en acier inoxydable, faire chauffer l'huile à feu moyen. Cuire les oignons 5 minutes.

3. Ajouter l'ail, le céleri, les carottes, les poivrons et les piments bananes dans la casserole. Cuire 5 minutes.

4. Ajouter le reste des ingrédients. Porter à ébullition, puis laisser mijoter 5 minutes à feu doux-moyen. Goûter et rectifier l'assaisonnement au besoin.

5. Répartir le chili dans les bocaux, en laissant un espace libre de 2,5 cm (1 po) entre le chili et le rebord des pots.

6. Plonger un ustensile dans les pots et le remuer afin d'éliminer toute bulle d'air. Au besoin, ajouter du chili.

7. Stériliser à l'autoclave (65 minutes pour des pots de 250 ml, 75 minutes pour des pots de 500 ml et 90 minutes pour des pots de 1 litre) selon les indications de la page 20.

! À servir bien chaud, garni de fromage et de coriandre fraîche! On peut faire de ce chili une version plus classique en remplaçant la viande de dinde par 2,7 kg (6 lb) de bœuf haché cru qu'on fera dorer avant d'ajouter les légumes.

Cassoulet au canard

PAR PORTION 1 pot de 500 ml	
Calories	1985
Protéines	109 g
M.G.	166 g
Glucides	45 g
Fibres	8 g
Fer	11 mg
Calcium	166 mg
Sodium	1866 mg

STÉRILISATION

QUANTITÉ TOTALE • 2,5 LITRES (10 TASSES)

Taille des pots	Temps de stérilisation
250 ml (8 oz)	65 minutes
500 ml (16 oz)	75 minutes
1 litre (32 oz)	90 minutes

À l'autoclave

Préparation
40 minutes

Trempage
12 heures

Réfrigération
4 heures

Cuisson
34 minutes

- **sans œuf**
- **sans produits laitiers**
- **sans noix**
- **sans gluten**

250 ml (1 tasse) de haricots blancs secs (200 g)

2 tranches de bacon hachées (80 g)

500 g (1,1 lb) de saucisses Toulouse coupées en rondelles de 2,5 cm (1 po)

250 ml (1 tasse) d'oignon haché (140 g)

250 ml (1 tasse) de carotte coupée en rondelles de 1 cm – ½ po (140 g)

4 gousses d'ail hachées (20 g)

60 ml (¼ de tasse) de sirop d'érable

1,25 ml (¼ de c. à thé) de clous de girofle moulus

4 baies de genièvre écrasées

2 feuilles de laurier émiettées

Sel et poivre au goût

Pour le canard :

1 canard entier surgelé de 2,56 kg (5,6 lb)

4 litres (8 tasses) d'eau froide

1 carotte entière avec les fanes (90 g)

1 branche de céleri entière avec les feuilles (40 g)

1 gousse d'ail (5 g)

½ oignon (65 g)

1. La veille, faire tremper les haricots dans 750 ml (3 tasses) d'eau froide de 12 à 18 heures au frais.

2. Déposer le canard entier congelé dans l'autoclave. Ajouter l'eau et le reste des ingrédients pour le canard dans l'autoclave. Saler et poivrer, puis visser le couvercle. Allumer le feu à élevé et placer la pesée de 15 psi sur la soupape d'évacuation (peu importe l'altitude). Il n'est pas nécessaire de laisser l'autoclave ventiler 10 minutes.

3. À partir du moment où la pesée se met à bouger, cuire 20 minutes, en s'assurant de maintenir la pression à 15 psi. Éteindre le feu et laisser la pression retomber d'elle-même.

4. Désosser le canard, puis défaire la chair en morceaux. Réserver au frais.

5. À l'aide d'une passoire fine, filter le bouillon contenu dans l'autoclave au-dessus d'un bol, puis le laisser reposer au frais 4 heures, jusqu'à ce que le gras fige à la surface. Jeter les légumes.

6. Au moment de la mise en conserve, égoutter les haricots et jeter l'eau de trempage. Rincer les haricots à l'eau froide et égoutter de nouveau. Réserver. Retirer le gras de canard à la surface du bouillon.

7. Dans une grande casserole en acier inoxydable, cuire le bacon et les rondelles de saucisses de 3 à 4 minutes à feu moyen. Réserver dans une assiette.

8. Dans la même casserole, cuire l'oignon et la carotte 5 minutes à feu moyen.

9. Ajouter l'ail et poursuivre la cuisson 1 minute.

10. Déglacer avec 1 litre (4 tasses) du bouillon de canard réservé, en raclant le fond de la casserole avec une cuillère en bois afin de détacher les sucs de cuisson.

11. Ajouter la viande de canard cuite, les haricots et le reste des ingrédients. Porter à ébullition, puis laisser mijoter 5 minutes à feu doux-moyen.

12. À l'aide d'une cuillère trouée, répartir les aliments solides dans les bocaux, en laissant un espace libre de 3,5 cm (1 ½ po) entre les aliments et le rebord des pots.

13. Transvider le bouillon dans une casserole en acier inoxydable et porter à ébullition.

14. Verser le bouillon bouillant dans les bocaux, en laissant un espace libre de 2,5 cm (1 po) entre le bouillon et le rebord des pots.

15. Plonger un ustensile dans les pots et le remuer afin d'éliminer toute bulle d'air. Au besoin, ajouter du bouillon.

16. Stériliser à l'autoclave (65 minutes pour des pots de 250 ml, 75 minutes pour des pots de 500 ml et 90 minutes pour des pots de 1 litre) selon les indications de la page 20.

! S'il vous reste du bouillon après avoir réalisé la recette, il est possible de le mettre en conserve en suivant les mêmes temps de stérilisation selon les différents formats de pots de la recette de dinde congelée et son bouillon de la page 40.

Poulet au cidre et aux pommes

PAR PORTION 1 pot de 500 ml	
Calories	438
Protéines	54 g
M.G.	13 g
Glucides	25 g
Fibres	3 g
Fer	1 mg
Calcium	34 mg
Sodium	755 mg

STÉRILISATION

QUANTITÉ TOTALE • 1 LITRE (4 TASSES)

Taille des pots	Temps de stérilisation
250 ml (8 oz)	65 minutes
500 ml (16 oz)	75 minutes
1 litre (32 oz)	90 minutes

À l'autoclave

Préparation
20 minutes

Cuisson
17 minutes

- **sans œuf**
- **sans noix**
- **sans gluten**

15 ml (1 c. à soupe) d'huile végétale

450 g (1 lb) de poitrines de poulet sans peau coupées en lanières de 1 cm (½ po) d'épaisseur

80 ml (⅓ de tasse) d'échalotes sèches (françaises) hachées (40 g)

½ contenant de champignons de 227 g, coupés en quartiers

1 gousse d'ail hachée (5 g)

1 pomme Cortland (ou une pomme à chair ferme) épépinée et coupée en quartiers (180 g)

125 ml (½ tasse) de cidre de pomme non effervescent

375 ml (1 ½ tasse) de bouillon de dinde (voir recette à la page 40)

Sel et poivre au goût

1. Dans une grande casserole en acier inoxydable, chauffer l'huile à feu moyen-élevé. Faire dorer les lanières de poulet de 4 à 5 minutes, jusqu'à ce que l'intérieur de la chair du poulet ait perdu sa teinte rosée.

2. Ajouter les échalotes et les champignons dans la casserole. Poursuivre la cuisson 7 minutes.

3. Ajouter l'ail et les quartiers de pomme. Poursuivre la cuisson 1 minute.

4. Déglacer avec le cidre, en raclant le fond de la casserole avec une cuillère en bois afin de détacher les sucs de cuisson.

5. Verser le bouillon. Saler et poivrer. Porter à ébullition, puis laisser mijoter 5 minutes à feu doux-moyen. Goûter et rectifier l'assaisonnement au besoin.

6. À l'aide d'une cuillère trouée, répartir les aliments solides dans les bocaux, en laissant un espace libre de 2,5 cm (1 po) entre les aliments et le rebord des pots.

7. Verser le bouillon bouillant dans les bocaux, en laissant un espace libre de 2,5 cm (1 po) entre le bouillon et le rebord des pots.

8. Plonger un ustensile dans les pots et le remuer afin d'éliminer toute bulle d'air. Au besoin, ajouter du bouillon.

9. Stériliser à l'autoclave (65 minutes pour des pots de 250 ml, 75 minutes pour des pots de 500 ml et 90 minutes pour un pot de 1 litre) selon les indications de la page 20.

! Au moment de servir, si vous le désirez, épaississez la sauce avec un peu de crème à cuisson. Pour ce faire, il suffit de verser le bouillon dans une casserole, d'ajouter de la crème à cuisson 15% (40 ml – 8 c. à thé pour un pot de 250 ml, 80 ml – ⅓ de tasse pour un pot de 500 ml, ou 160 ml – ⅔ de tasse pour un pot de 1 litre) et de la fécule de maïs (2,5 ml – ½ c. à thé pour un pot de 250 ml, 5 ml – 1 c. à thé pour un pot de 500 ml, et 10 ml – 2 c. à thé pour un pot de 1 litre), puis de réchauffer quelques minutes en remuant.

PAR PORTION 1 pot de 500 ml	
Calories	525
Protéines	76 g
M.G.	13 g
Glucides	48 g
Fibres	7 g
Fer	5 mg
Calcium	95 mg
Sodium	1601 mg

Pulled turkey

STÉRILISATION

QUANTITÉ TOTALE • 1 LITRE (4 TASSES)

Taille des pots	Temps de stérilisation
250 ml (8 oz)	65 minutes
500 ml (16 oz)	75 minutes
1 litre (32 oz)	90 minutes

À l'autoclave

Préparation
5 minutes

Cuisson
5 minutes

- **sans œuf**
- **sans produits laitiers**
- **sans noix**

450 g (1 lb) de viande de dinde cuite (voir recette à la page 40)

500 ml (2 tasses) de sauce barbecue fumée aux pommes (voir recette à la page 96)

1. Dans une casserole en acier inoxydable, déposer la viande et la sauce barbecue. Porter à ébullition à feu doux.

2. Effilocher la viande dans la sauce à l'aide d'une fourchette.

3. Répartir l'effiloché de dinde bouillant dans les bocaux, en laissant un espace libre de 2,5 cm (1 po) entre la viande et le rebord des pots.

4. Plonger un ustensile dans les pots et le remuer afin d'éliminer toute bulle d'air. Au besoin, ajouter de la viande.

5. Stériliser à l'autoclave (65 minutes pour des pots de 250 ml, 75 minutes pour des pots de 500 ml et 90 minutes pour un pot de 1 litre) selon les indications de la page 20.

PAR PORTION 1 pot de 500 ml	
Calories	412
Protéines	45 g
M.G.	18 g
Glucides	32 g
Fibres	6 g
Fer	5 mg
Calcium	91 mg
Sodium	608 mg

Dinde en sauce *mole*

STÉRILISATION

QUANTITÉ TOTALE • 2 LITRES (8 TASSES)

Taille des pots	Temps de stérilisation
250 ml (8 oz)	65 minutes
500 ml (16 oz)	75 minutes
1 litre (32 oz)	90 minutes

À l'autoclave

Préparation
35 minutes

Cuisson
15 minutes

- **sans œuf**
- **sans produits laitiers**
- **sans gluten**

15 ml (1 c. à soupe) d'huile végétale

250 ml (1 tasse) d'oignon haché (140 g)

3 gousses d'ail hachées (15 g)

80 ml (⅓ de tasse) de raisins secs (80 g)

1 jalapeño épépiné et haché (40 g)

15 ml (1 c. à soupe) de cacao

60 g (environ 2 oz) de chocolat noir 70 % sans lactose haché

60 ml (¼ de tasse) de poudre d'amandes (18 g)

15 ml (1 c. à soupe) de chipotle (facultatif)

2,5 ml (½ c. à thé) de cumin

5 ml (1 c. à thé) de cannelle

30 ml (2 c. à soupe) de pâte de tomates

500 ml (2 tasses) de coulis de tomates (voir recette à la page 28)

500 ml (2 tasses) de bouillon de dinde (voir recette à la page 40)

Sel et poivre au goût

1 litre (4 tasses) de viande de dinde (500 g) coupée en dés (voir recette à la page 40)

1. Dans une grande casserole en acier inoxydable, chauffer l'huile à feu moyen. Cuire l'oignon, l'ail, les raisins secs et le jalapeño de 5 à 7 minutes.

2. Ajouter le cacao, le chocolat, la poudre d'amandes, les épices, la pâte de tomates, le coulis de tomates et le bouillon de dinde dans la casserole. Saler et poivrer. Porter à ébullition, puis laisser mijoter 10 minutes à feu doux, en remuant à l'occasion.

3. À l'aide du mélangeur à main, mélanger la préparation hors du feu jusqu'à l'obtention d'une préparation lisse et onctueuse. Goûter et rectifier l'assaisonnement au besoin.

4. Ajouter la viande de dinde dans la casserole et porter de nouveau à ébullition.

5. À l'aide d'une cuillère trouée, répartir la viande dans les bocaux, en laissant un espace libre de 2,5 cm (1 po) entre la viande et le rebord des pots.

6. Verser la sauce bouillante dans les bocaux, en laissant un espace libre de 2,5 cm (1 po) entre la sauce et le rebord des pots.

7. Plonger un ustensile dans les pots et le remuer afin d'éliminer toute bulle d'air. Au besoin, ajouter de la sauce.

8. Stériliser à l'autoclave (65 minutes pour des pots de 250 ml, 75 minutes pour des pots de 500 ml et 90 minutes pour des pots de 1 litre) selon les indications de la page 20.

PAR PORTION 1 pot de 500 ml	
Calories	461
Protéines	49 g
M.G.	17 g
Glucides	20 g
Fibres	6 g
Fer	6 mg
Calcium	88 mg
Sodium	691 mg

Poulet cacciatore

STÉRILISATION

QUANTITÉ TOTALE • 1,5 LITRE (6 TASSES)

Taille des pots	Temps de stérilisation
250 ml (8 oz)	65 minutes
500 ml (16 oz)	75 minutes
1 litre (32 oz)	90 minutes

À l'autoclave

Préparation
25 minutes

Cuisson
10 minutes

- **sans œuf**
- **sans produits laitiers**
- **sans noix**
- **sans gluten**

15 ml (1 c. à soupe) d'huile végétale

680 g (1 ½ lb) de hauts de cuisses de poulet désossés et sans peau, coupés en dés de 2,5 cm (1 po)

250 ml (1 tasse) de champignons coupés en quartiers (114 g)

375 ml (1 ½ tasse) de poivrons rouges coupés en lanières (210 g)

125 ml (½ tasse) d'oignon haché (70 g)

1 gousse d'ail hachée (5 g)

125 ml (½ tasse) de vin blanc

500 ml (2 tasses) de coulis de tomates (voir recette à la page 28)

250 ml (1 tasse) de bouillon de dinde (voir recette à la page 40)

125 ml (½ tasse) d'olives noires dénoyautées (60 g)

15 ml (1 c. à soupe) de persil frais haché (4 g)

Sel et poivre au goût

1. Dans une grande casserole en acier inoxydable, chauffer l'huile à feu élevé. Faire dorer les dés de poulet, les champignons, les poivrons et l'oignon de 4 à 5 minutes, jusqu'à ce que l'intérieur de la chair du poulet ait perdu sa teinte rosée.

2. Ajouter l'ail dans la casserole. Remuer et poursuivre la cuisson 1 minute.

3. Déglacer avec le vin blanc, en raclant le fond de la casserole avec une cuillère en bois afin de détacher les sucs de cuisson.

4. Ajouter le reste des ingrédients et laisser mijoter 5 minutes à feu doux.

5. À l'aide d'une cuillère trouée, répartir les aliments solides dans les bocaux, en laissant un espace libre de 2,5 cm (1 po) entre les aliments et le rebord des pots.

6. Verser la sauce dans les pots, en laissant un espace libre de 2,5 cm (1 po) entre la sauce et le rebord des pots.

7. Plonger un ustensile dans les pots et le remuer afin d'éliminer toute bulle d'air. Au besoin, ajouter de la sauce.

8. Stériliser à l'autoclave (65 minutes pour des pots de 250 ml, 75 minutes pour des pots de 500 ml et 90 minutes pour des pots de 1 litre) selon les indications de la page 20.

PAR PORTION 1 pot de 500 ml	
Calories	1005
Protéines	69 g
M.G.	71 g
Glucides	14 g
Fibres	2 g
Fer	4 mg
Calcium	69 mg
Sodium	2214 mg

Hauts de cuisses jerk

STÉRILISATION

QUANTITÉ TOTALE • 1,5 LITRE (6 TASSES)

Taille des pots	Temps de stérilisation
250 ml (8 oz)	65 minutes
500 ml (16 oz)	75 minutes
1 litre (32 oz)	90 minutes

À l'autoclave

Préparation
25 minutes

Cuisson
11 minutes

- **sans œuf**
- **sans produits laitiers**
- **sans noix**

6 hauts de cuisses de poulet avec os et peau coupés en deux (1,2 kg)

15 ml (1 c. à soupe) de mélange d'épices jerk (voir recette à la page 42)

15 ml (1 c. à soupe) d'huile végétale

1 oignon coupé en deux (140 g)

1 jalapeño épépiné et coupé en deux (40 g)

60 ml (¼ de tasse) de sauce soya

60 ml (¼ de tasse) de vinaigre de cidre

500 ml (2 tasses) de bouillon de dinde (voir recette à la page 40)

15 ml (1 c. à soupe) de cassonade

Sel et poivre au goût

1. Dans un bol, déposer les hauts de cuisses et la moitié du mélange d' épices jerk. Remuer pour bien enrober les hauts de cuisses d'épices jerk.

2. Dans une grande poêle, chauffer l'huile à feu élevé. Cuire les hauts de cuisse de 3 à 5 minutes de chaque côté, jusqu'à ce que l'intérieur de la chair du poulet ait perdu sa teinte rosée.

3. Déposer les hauts de cuisses dans les pots (1 haut de cuisse pour des pots de 250 ml, 2 hauts de cuisses pour des pots de 500 ml et 4 hauts de cuisses pour des pots de 1 litre).

4. Dans le contenant du mélangeur électrique, déposer le reste des ingrédients. Mélanger jusqu'à l'obtention d'une préparation lisse.

5. Transvider la préparation dans une casserole en acier inoxydable. Porter à ébullition, puis laisser mijoter 5 minutes à feu moyen, en remuant fréquemment.

6. Verser la sauce dans les bocaux, en laissant un espace libre de 2,5 cm (1 po) entre la sauce et le rebord des pots.

7. Plonger un ustensile dans les pots et le remuer afin d'éliminer toute bulle d'air. Au besoin, ajouter de la sauce.

8. Stériliser à l'autoclave (65 minutes pour des pots de 250 ml, 75 minutes pour des pots de 500 ml et 90 minutes pour des pots de 1 litre) selon les indications de la page 20.

! Au moment de servir, videz le contenu d'un pot dans un plat de cuisson, la peau des hauts de cuisses vers le haut. Réchauffez la préparation au four de 30 à 40 minutes à 205°C (400°F), jusqu'à ce que la peau des hauts de cuisses soit croustillante. Notez également qu'il sera plus facile de manier les hauts de cuisses de cette recette s'ils sont déposés dans des pots à large ouverture.

PORC

Le porc est ma viande préférée, celle que je consomme le plus à la maison et en conserve. On produit un porc d'une excellente qualité au Québec. En plus, il s'agit d'une viande moins chère et moins polluante que le bœuf. Découvrez dans cette section une multitude de recettes à base de porc pour égayer vos papilles !

Cari de porc au lait de coco

PAR PORTION 1 pot de 500 ml	
Calories	436
Protéines	38 g
M.G.	22 g
Glucides	23 g
Fibres	4 g
Fer	3 mg
Calcium	85 mg
Sodium	1050 mg

STÉRILISATION

QUANTITÉ TOTALE • 3 LITRES (12 TASSES)

Taille des pots	Temps de stérilisation
250 ml (8 oz)	65 minutes
500 ml (16 oz)	75 minutes
1 litre (32 oz)	90 minutes

À l'autoclave

Préparation
25 minutes

Cuisson
17 minutes

- **sans œuf**
- **sans produits laitiers**
- **sans gluten**

45 ml (3 c. à soupe) d'huile de coco ou d'huile végétale

2 lb (environ 900 g) de longe de porc, le gras enlevé, coupée en dés de 2,5 cm (1 po)

250 ml (1 tasse) d'oignon haché (140 g)

30 ml (2 c. à soupe) de poudre de cari

2 gousses d'ail hachées (10 g)

1 piment thaï haché finement, facultatif (5 g)

1,5 litre (6 tasses) de bouillon de dinde (voir recette à la page 40)

1 boîte de lait de coco non sucré de 160 ml

1 litre (4 tasses) de courge Butternut coupée en dés de 1 cm – ½ po (550 g)

250 ml (1 tasse) de pois verts frais ou surgelés (120 g)

250 ml (1 tasse) de haricots verts coupés en tronçons de 2,5 cm (1 po) de longueur (150 g)

Sel et poivre au goût

1. Dans une grande casserole en acier inoxydable, chauffer l'huile à feu moyen-élevé. Faire dorer les dés de porc de 4 à 5 minutes sur toutes les faces.

2. Ajouter l'oignon et la poudre de cari dans la casserole. Cuire 7 minutes à feu moyen en remuant.

3. Ajouter l'ail et le piment thaï. Poursuivre la cuisson 1 minute en remuant.

4. Déglacer avec le bouillon, en raclant le fond de la casserole avec une cuillère en bois afin de détacher les sucs de cuisson. Porter à ébullition.

5. Ajouter le lait de coco, les dés de courge, les pois verts et les haricots. Saler, poivrer et laisser mijoter 5 minutes à feu doux. Goûter et rectifier l'assaisonnement au besoin.

6. À l'aide d'une cuillère trouée, répartir les aliments solides dans les bocaux, en laissant un espace libre de 2,5 cm (1 po) entre les aliments et le rebord des pots.

7. Verser le bouillon bouillant dans les bocaux, en laissant un espace libre de 2,5 cm (1 po) entre le bouillon et le rebord des pots.

8. Plonger un ustensile dans les pots et le remuer afin d'éliminer toute bulle d'air. Au besoin, ajouter du bouillon.

9. Stériliser à l'autoclave (65 minutes pour des pots de 250 ml, 75 minutes pour des pots de 500 ml et 90 minutes pour des pots de 1 litre) selon les indications de la page 20.

! Il est important de ne pas augmenter la proportion de lait de coco par rapport au bouillon lors de la mise en conserve de cette recette. Si vous aimez un cari plus crémeux, ajoutez du lait de coco au moment de servir seulement.

Ragoût de boulettes de Noël

PAR PORTION 1 pot de 500 ml	
Calories	675
Protéines	75 g
M.G.	40 g
Glucides	10 g
Fibres	2 g
Fer	4 mg
Calcium	58 mg
Sodium	1270 mg

STÉRILISATION

QUANTITÉ TOTALE • 6 LITRES (24 TASSES)

Taille des pots	Temps de stérilisation
500 ml (16 oz)	75 minutes
1 litre (32 oz)	90 minutes

À l'autoclave

Préparation
45 minutes

Temps de repos
10 minutes

Cuisson
10 minutes

- **sans produits laitiers**
- **sans noix**

3 litres (12 tasses) de bouillon de dinde (voir recette à la page 40)

2 litres (8 tasses) de viande de dinde cuite (1,45 kg) coupée en morceaux (voir recette à la page 40)

360 ml (1 ⅓ tasse + 2 c. à soupe) de farine

Pour les boulettes:

125 ml (½ tasse) d'eau bouillante

250 ml (1 tasse) de son d'avoine (120 g)

2 œufs

2,72 kg (6 lb) de porc haché maigre

250 ml (1 tasse) d'oignon haché (140 g)

250 ml (1 tasse) de céleri haché (140 g)

15 ml (1 c. à soupe) de moutarde en poudre

15 ml (1 c. à soupe) de sel

15 ml (1 c. à soupe) de moutarde de Dijon

10 ml (2 c. à thé) de poivre

10 ml (2 c. à thé) de clous de girofle moulus

10 ml (2 c. à thé) de cannelle

1. Dans un bol, mélanger l'eau bouillante avec le son d'avoine. Laisser gonfler 10 minutes.

2. Préchauffer le four à 260 °C (500 °F).

3. Dans un grand bol, fouetter les œufs. Ajouter le son d'avoine et le reste des ingrédients pour les boulettes dans le bol. Bien mélanger.

4. Façonner des boulettes de 2,5 cm (1 po) de diamètre avec la préparation au porc, puis les déposer sur une plaque de cuisson tapissée de papier parchemin. Cuire au four 10 minutes.

5. Dans une casserole en acier inoxydable, porter le bouillon de dinde à ébullition.

6. Répartir la viande de dinde et les boulettes dans les bocaux, en laissant un espace libre de 3,5 cm (1 ½ po) entre les aliments et le rebord des pots.

7. Verser le bouillon bouillant dans les bocaux, en laissant un espace libre de 2,5 cm (1 po) entre le bouillon et le rebord des pots.

8. Plonger un ustensile dans les pots et le remuer afin d'éliminer toute bulle d'air. Au besoin, ajouter du bouillon.

9. Stériliser à l'autoclave (75 minutes pour des pots de 500 ml ou 90 minutes pour des pots de 1 litre) selon les indications de la page 20.

10. Au moment de servir, faire griller la farine (30 ml – 2 c. à soupe pour un pot de 500 ml ou 60 ml – ¼ de tasse pour un pot de 1 litre) dans une casserole en acier inoxydable à feu moyen. Verser graduellement le bouillon dans la casserole en remuant constamment, jusqu'à épaississement.

11. Ajouter la viande et les boulettes dans la casserole et laisser mijoter à feu doux-moyen, jusqu'à ce que le ragoût soit bien chaud.

! Je prépare cette recette en novembre, quand le porc et la dinde sont à prix réduits dans les épiceries. Je commence par cuire la dinde selon la technique de la page 40 le premier jour, puis je fais les boulettes et la stérilisation le lendemain. Je double, et même triple la recette: elle est tellement bonne que j'en mange à l'année, pas juste à Noël!

PAR PORTION 1 pot de 500 ml	
Calories	779
Protéines	70 g
M.G.	40 g
Glucides	27 g
Fibres	6 g
Fer	3 mg
Calcium	119 mg
Sodium	1215 mg

Rôti de porc à l'oignon

STÉRILISATION

QUANTITÉ TOTALE • 1,5 LITRE (6 TASSES)

Taille des pots	Temps de stérilisation
250 ml (8 oz)	65 minutes
500 ml (16 oz)	75 minutes
1 litre (32 oz)	90 minutes

À l'autoclave

Préparation
25 minutes

Cuisson
13 minutes

- **sans œuf**
- **sans produits laitiers**
- **sans noix**
- **sans gluten**

750 ml (3 tasses) de carottes coupées en rondelles de 2,5 cm – 1 po (340 g)

45 ml (3 c. à soupe) d'huile végétale

750 ml (3 tasses) d'oignons coupés en demi-rondelles (390 g)

1 gousse d'ail hachée (5 g)

1 pincée de sel

125 ml (½ tasse) de vin blanc sec

900 g (2 lb) de rôti de porc, le gras enlevé, coupé en cubes de 2,5 cm (1 po)

750 ml (3 tasses) de bouillon au choix (voir recettes aux pages 30, 32 et 40)

15 ml (1 c. à soupe) de moutarde de Dijon

5 ml (1 c. à thé) de thym séché

1 feuille de laurier émiettée

Poivre au goût

1. Répartir les rondelles de carottes dans les pots.

2. Dans une grande casserole en acier inoxydable, chauffer la moitié de l'huile à feu doux-moyen. Déposer les oignons et l'ail dans la casserole. Saler. Cuire 5 minutes, jusqu'à ce que les oignons soient translucides.

3. Déglacer avec le vin blanc, en raclant le fond de la casserole avec une cuillère en bois afin de détacher les sucs de cuisson. Réserver.

4. Dans une grande poêle, chauffer le reste de l'huile à feu élevé. Saisir les cubes de porc de 3 à 4 minutes sur toutes les faces.

5. Déglacer avec 250 ml (1 tasse) de bouillon, en raclant le fond de la poêle avec une cuillère en bois afin de détacher les sucs de cuisson.

6. Ajouter le porc et le reste des ingrédients dans la casserole. Porter à ébullition, puis laisser mijoter 5 minutes à feu doux.

7. À l'aide d'une cuillère trouée, répartir les aliments solides dans les bocaux, en laissant un espace libre de 2,5 cm (1 po) entre les aliments et le rebord des pots.

8. Verser le bouillon bouillant dans les bocaux, en laissant un espace libre de 2,5 cm (1 po) entre le bouillon et le rebord des pots.

9. Plonger un ustensile dans les pots et le remuer afin d'éliminer toute bulle d'air. Au besoin, ajouter du bouillon.

10. Stériliser à l'autoclave (65 minutes pour des pots de 250 ml, 75 minutes pour des pots de 500 ml et 90 minutes pour des pots de 1 litre) selon les indications de la page 20.

PAR PORTION 1 pot de 500 ml	
Calories	545
Protéines	68 g
M.G.	21 g
Glucides	20 g
Fibres	5 g
Fer	5 mg
Calcium	104 mg
Sodium	588 mg

Longe de porc cajun

STÉRILISATION

QUANTITÉ TOTALE • 4,5 LITRES (18 TASSES)

Taille des pots	Temps de stérilisation
250 ml (8 oz)	65 minutes
500 ml (16 oz)	75 minutes
1 litre (32 oz)	90 minutes

À l'autoclave

Préparation
15 minutes

Cuisson
11 minutes

- **sans œuf**
- **sans produits laitiers**
- **sans noix**
- **sans gluten**

2,7 kg (6 lb) de longe de porc, le gras enlevé, coupée en lanières de 1 cm (½ po) d'épaisseur

125 ml (½ tasse) de mélange d'épices cajun (voir recette à la page 44)

30 ml (2 c. à soupe) d'huile végétale

1 litre (4 tasses) d'oignons hachés (560 g)

6 gousses d'ail hachées (30 g)

2 litres (8 tasses) de coulis de tomates (voir recette à la page 28)

1. Préchauffer le four à 260 °C (500 °F).

2. Déposer les lanières de porc sur une plaque de cuisson tapissée de papier parchemin. Saupoudrer de la moitié des épices cajun. Remuer pour bien enrober les lanières d'épices.

3. Cuire au four 10 minutes. Le porc n'a pas besoin d'être complètement cuit, car la cuisson se terminera dans l'autoclave.

4. Pendant ce temps, chauffer l'huile à feu moyen-élevé dans une casserole en acier inoxydable. Cuire les oignons 5 minutes, jusqu'à ce qu'ils soient translucides.

5. Ajouter l'ail et le reste des épices cajun dans la casserole. Cuire 1 minute.

6. Ajouter le coulis de tomates. Porter à ébullition, puis laisser mijoter 5 minutes à feu doux.

7. Répartir les lanières de porc dans les bocaux, en laissant un espace libre de 2,5 cm (1 po) entre la viande et le rebord des pots.

8. Verser la sauce bouillante dans les bocaux, en laissant un espace libre de 2,5 cm (1 po) entre la sauce et le rebord des pots.

9. Plonger un ustensile dans les pots et le remuer afin d'éliminer toute bulle d'air. Au besoin, ajouter de la sauce.

10. Stériliser à l'autoclave (65 minutes pour des pots de 250 ml, 75 minutes pour des pots de 500 ml et 90 minutes pour des pots de 1 litre) selon les indications de la page 20.

Casserole de jambon à gratiner

PAR PORTION 1 pot de 500 ml	
Calories	277
Protéines	27 g
M.G.	5 g
Glucides	30 g
Fibres	4 g
Fer	2 mg
Calcium	40 mg
Sodium	1400 mg

STÉRILISATION

QUANTITÉ TOTALE • 2 LITRES (8 TASSES)

Taille des pots	Temps de stérilisation
250 ml (8 oz)	65 minutes
500 ml (16 oz)	75 minutes
1 litre (32 oz)	90 minutes

À l'autoclave

Préparation
25 minutes

Cuisson
5 minutes

- **sans œuf**
- **sans noix**
- **sans gluten**

660 ml (2 ⅔ tasses) de pommes de terre Russet ou Yukon Gold (400 g)

1 litre (4 tasses) d'eau ou de bouillon au choix (voir recettes aux pages 30, 32 et 40)

500 g (environ 1 lb) de jambon Forêt-Noire coupé en dés de 2,5 cm (1 po)

250 ml (1 tasse) de carotte coupée en rondelles de 2,5 cm – 1 po (140 g)

250 ml (1 tasse) de pois verts surgelés (120 g)

Sel et poivre au goût

Fromage râpé au goût

1. Peler les pommes de terre, puis les couper en dés de 1 cm (½ po). Rincer les dés de pommes de terre à l'eau froide.

2. Dans une casserole en acier inoxydable, porter le bouillon à ébullition.

3. Répartir les dés de pommes de terre et le reste des ingrédients, à l'exception du fromage, dans les bocaux, en laissant un espace libre de 2,5 cm (1 po) entre les aliments et le rebord des pots.

4. Verser le bouillon bouillant dans les bocaux, en laissant un espace libre de 2,5 cm (1 po) entre le bouillon et le rebord des pots.

5. Plonger un ustensile dans les pots et le remuer afin d'éliminer toute bulle d'air. Au besoin, ajouter du bouillon.

6. Stériliser à l'autoclave (65 minutes pour des pots de 250 ml, 75 minutes pour des pots de 500 ml et 90 minutes pour des pots de 1 litre) selon les indications de la page 20.

7. Au moment de servir, égoutter le contenu d'un pot et jeter le liquide. Transvider les aliments solides dans un plat de cuisson et couvrir de fromage. Cuire au four 20 minutes à 205 °C (400 °F).

Filet de porc à la mangue

PAR PORTION 1 pot de 500 ml	
Calories	308
Protéines	40 g
M.G.	7 g
Glucides	19 g
Fibres	3 g
Fer	3 mg
Calcium	39 mg
Sodium	797 mg

STÉRILISATION

QUANTITÉ TOTALE • 3 LITRES (12 TASSES)

Taille des pots	Temps de stérilisation
250 ml (8 oz)	65 minutes
500 ml (16 oz)	75 minutes
1 litre (32 oz)	90 minutes

À l'autoclave

Préparation
25 minutes

Cuisson
11 minutes

- **sans œuf**
- **sans produits laitiers**
- **sans noix**
- **sans gluten**

1 kg (environ 2 ¼ lb) de filets de porc

30 ml (2 c. à soupe) d'huile végétale

250 ml (1 tasse) de poivron rouge coupé en dés de 2,5 cm – 1 po (200 g)

250 ml (1 tasse) de poivron vert coupé en dés de 2,5 cm – 1 po (200 g)

250 ml (1 tasse) d'oignon coupé en dés de 2,5 cm – 1 po (140 g)

375 ml (1 ½ tasse) de mangue coupée en dés (500 g)

2 gousses d'ail hachées (10 g)

60 ml (¼ de tasse) de vinaigre de cidre

1 litre (4 tasses) de bouillon de dinde (voir recette à la page 40)

15 ml (1 c. à soupe) de sauce soya

5 ml (1 c. à thé) de flocons de piment (facultatif, au goût)

Sel et poivre au goût

1. Parer les filets de porc en retirant la membrane blanche. Couper les filets de porc en deux sur la longueur, puis en demi-rondelles de 1 cm (½ po) d'épaisseur.

2. Dans une casserole en acier inoxydable, chauffer l'huile à feu élevé. Faire dorer les morceaux de porc de 3 à 4 minutes sur toutes les faces.

3. Répartir les morceaux de porc dans les pots.

4. Dans la même casserole, cuire les légumes et la mangue 5 minutes à feu moyen.

5. Ajouter l'ail et poursuivre la cuisson 1 minute en remuant.

6. Déglacer avec le vinaigre de cidre, en raclant le fond de la casserole avec une cuillère en bois afin de détacher les sucs de cuisson.

7. Ajouter le reste des ingrédients dans la casserole. Porter à ébullition, puis laisser mijoter 2 minutes à feu moyen.

8. À l'aide d'une cuillère trouée, répartir les aliments solides dans les bocaux, en laissant un espace libre de 2,5 cm (1 po) entre les aliments et le rebord des pots.

9. Verser le bouillon bouillant dans les bocaux, en laissant un espace libre de 2,5 cm (1 po) entre le bouillon et le rebord des pots.

10. Plonger un ustensile dans les pots et le remuer afin d'éliminer toute bulle d'air. Au besoin, ajouter du bouillon.

11. Stériliser à l'autoclave (65 minutes pour des pots de 250 ml, 75 minutes pour des pots de 500 ml et 90 minutes pour des pots de 1 litre) selon les indications de la page 20.

Boulettes de viande cajuns

PAR PORTION 1 pot de 500 ml	
Calories	521
Protéines	42 g
M.G.	32 g
Glucides	17 g
Fibres	4 g
Fer	4 mg
Calcium	61 mg
Sodium	236 mg

STÉRILISATION

QUANTITÉ TOTALE • 8 LITRES (32 TASSES)

Taille des pots	Temps de stérilisation
250 ml (8 oz)	65 minutes
500 ml (16 oz)	75 minutes
1 litre (32 oz)	90 minutes

À l'autoclave

Préparation
40 minutes

Temps de repos
10 minutes

Cuisson
10 minutes

- **sans produits laitiers**
- **sans noix**

125 ml (½ tasse) d'eau bouillante

250 ml (1 tasse) de son d'avoine (120 g)

3 branches de céleri coupées en tronçons (330 g)

1 gros oignon coupé en quartiers (140 g)

4 gousses d'ail (20 g)

3,2 kg (environ 7 lb) de porc haché maigre

2 œufs battus

250 ml (1 tasse) de mélange d'épices cajun (voir recette à la page 44)

3 litres (12 tasses) de coulis de tomates (voir recette à la page 28)

1. Dans un bol, mélanger l'eau bouillante avec le son d'avoine. Laisser gonfler 10 minutes.

2. Dans le contenant du robot culinaire, déposer le céleri, l'oignon et l'ail. Mélanger jusqu'à ce que les légumes soient hachés finement.

3. Dans un grand bol, mélanger la préparation à l'avoine avec les légumes hachés, le porc haché, les œufs battus et la moitié des épices cajun.

4. Préchauffer le four à 260 °C (500 °F).

5. Façonner des boulettes de 2,5 cm (1 po) de diamètre avec la préparation à la viande, puis les déposer sur deux plaques de cuisson tapissées de papier parchemin. Cuire au four 10 minutes.

6. Répartir les boulettes dans les bocaux, en laissant un espace libre de 2,5 cm (1 po) entre les boulettes et le rebord des pots.

7. Dans une casserole en acier inoxydable, mélanger le coulis de tomates avec le reste des épices cajun. Porter à ébullition. Si le coulis est très épais, il est possible de le délayer avec un peu d'eau.

8. Verser le coulis bouillant dans les bocaux, en laissant un espace libre de 2,5 cm (1 po) entre le coulis et le rebord des pots.

9. Plonger un ustensile dans les pots et le remuer afin d'éliminer toute bulle d'air. Au besoin, ajouter du coulis.

10. Stériliser à l'autoclave (65 minutes pour des pots de 250 ml, 75 minutes pour des pots de 500 ml et 90 minutes pour des pots de 1 litre) selon les indications de la page 20.

! Je mélange la préparation à la viande à l'aide d'un batteur sur socle, et j'utilise une cuillère à crème glacée pour façonner les boulettes afin de travailler plus rapidement. Je travaille aussi avec deux plaques de cuisson pour les boulettes: pendant que la première plaque est au four, je prépare la seconde.

BŒUF ET CIE

La sauce à spag et les boulettes sont probablement les plus grands classiques de la bouffe maison et les recettes les plus demandées pour la mise en conserve avec de la viande. Je vous ai donc préparé quelques incontournables, mais aussi des recettes différentes rehaussées de saveurs à découvrir.

PAR PORTION 1 pot de 500 ml	
Calories	621
Protéines	58 g
M.G.	30 g
Glucides	20 g
Fibres	4 g
Fer	6 mg
Calcium	79 mg
Sodium	848 mg

Bœuf à la bière

STÉRILISATION

QUANTITÉ TOTALE • 2 LITRES (8 TASSES)

Taille des pots	**Temps de stérilisation**
250 ml (8 oz)	65 minutes
500 ml (16 oz)	75 minutes
1 litre (32 oz)	90 minutes

À l'autoclave

Préparation
20 minutes

Cuisson
16 minutes

• sans œuf
• sans produits laitiers
• sans noix

45 ml (3 c. à soupe) d'huile végétale

1 kg (environ 2 ¼ lb) de cubes de bœuf à ragoût

250 ml (1 tasse) d'oignon coupé en dés (140 g)

375 ml (1 ½ tasse) de carottes coupées en rondelles de 1 cm – ½ po (170 g)

½ contenant de champignons de Paris de 227 g, tranchés

250 ml (1 tasse) de haricots verts coupés en tronçons de 2,5 cm – 1 po (115 g)

3 gousses d'ail hachées (15 g)

60 ml (¼ de tasse) de vinaigre de vin rouge

1 bouteille de bière de 375 ml

500 ml (2 tasses) de bouillon de bœuf (voir recette à la page 30)

30 ml (2 c. à soupe) de pâte de tomates

7,5 ml (½ c. à soupe) de sirop d'érable

7,5 ml (½ c. à soupe) de moutarde de Dijon

7,5 ml (½ c. à soupe) de moutarde à l'ancienne

0,625 ml (⅛ de c. à thé) de raifort

1 feuille de laurier émiettée

60 ml (¼ de tasse) de fécule de maïs

1. Dans une grande poêle à haut rebord, chauffer 30 ml (2 c. à soupe) d'huile à feu moyen. Faire dorer les cubes de bœuf sur toutes les faces de 4 à 5 minutes.

2. Répartir la viande dans les pots.

3. Dans la même poêle, chauffer le reste de l'huile à feu moyen. Cuire l'oignon, les carottes, les champignons, les haricots et l'ail de 2 à 3 minutes.

4. Répartir les légumes dans les pots, en laissant un espace libre de 2,5 cm (1 po) entre les légumes et le rebord des pots.

5. Déglacer avec le vinaigre de vin rouge, en raclant le fond de la poêle avec une cuillère en bois afin de détacher les sucs de cuisson. Laisser mijoter jusqu'à réduction presque complète du liquide.

6. Ajouter la bière, le bouillon, la pâte de tomates, le sirop d'érable, la moutarde de Dijon, la moutarde à l'ancienne, le raifort et la feuille de laurier. Laisser mijoter 10 minutes à feu doux-moyen, jusqu'à ce que la bière ne pétille plus.

7. Verser le bouillon bouillant dans les bocaux, en laissant un espace libre de 2,5 cm (1 po) entre le bouillon et le rebord des pots.

8. Plonger un ustensile dans les pots et le remuer afin d'éliminer toute bulle d'air. Au besoin, ajouter du bouillon.

9. Stériliser à l'autoclave (65 minutes pour des pots de 250 ml, 75 minutes pour des pots de 500 ml et 90 minutes pour des pots de 1 litre) selon les indications de la page 20.

10. Au moment de servir, mélanger le bouillon contenu dans un pot avec la fécule de maïs (7,5 ml – ½ c. à soupe pour chaque pot de 250 ml, 15 ml – 1 c. à soupe pour chaque pot de 500 ml ou 30 ml – 2 c. à soupe pour chaque pot de 1 litre) dans une casserole, hors du feu. Porter à ébullition à feu moyen en fouettant, jusqu'à épaississement.

11. Ajouter les légumes et la viande dans la casserole. Remuer.

Rôti de palette de bœuf à l'asiatique

PAR PORTION 1 pot de 500 ml	
Calories	1096
Protéines	97 g
M.G.	59 g
Glucides	37 g
Fibres	1 g
Fer	11 mg
Calcium	88 mg
Sodium	2975 mg

STÉRILISATION

QUANTITÉ TOTALE • 1 LITRE (4 TASSES)

Taille des pots	Temps de stérilisation
250 ml (8 oz)	65 minutes
500 ml (16 oz)	75 minutes
1 litre (32 oz)	90 minutes

Préparation
15 minutes

Cuisson
3 minutes

- sans produits laitiers
- sans œuf
- sans gluten

60 ml (¼ de tasse) d'huile de sésame grillé

900 g (2 lb) de rôti de palette de bœuf coupé en cubes de 2,5 cm (1 po)

3 gousses d'ail hachées (15 g)

60 ml (¼ de tasse) de vinaigre de riz

250 ml (1 tasse) de bouillon de bœuf (voir recette à la page 30)

60 ml (¼ de tasse) de sauce hoisin

60 ml (¼ de tasse) de sauce soya

15 ml (1 c. à soupe) de sirop d'érable (ou de miel ou de sucre)

15 ml (1 c. à soupe) de gingembre haché

15 ml (1 c. à soupe) de sauce piquante (au goût, facultatif)

1. Dans une grande poêle à haut rebord, chauffer l'huile à feu élevé. Faire dorer les cubes de bœuf sur toutes les faces de 2 à 3 minutes. Retirer du feu et laisser reposer quelques minutes.

2. Répartir le bœuf dans les bocaux, en laissant un espace libre de 2,5 cm (1 po) entre la viande et le rebord des pots.

3. Dans la même poêle, cuire l'ail 30 secondes à feu moyen-élevé.

4. Déglacer avec le vinaigre de riz, en raclant le fond de la poêle avec une cuillère en bois afin de détacher les sucs de cuisson.

5. Ajouter le reste des ingrédients dans la poêle et porter à ébullition.

6. Verser le liquide bouillant dans les bocaux, en laissant un espace libre de 2,5 cm (1 po) entre le liquide et le rebord des pots.

7. Plonger un ustensile dans les pots et le remuer afin d'éliminer toute bulle d'air. Au besoin, ajouter du liquide.

8. Stériliser à l'autoclave (65 minutes pour des pots de 250 ml, 75 minutes pour des pots de 500 ml et 90 minutes pour des pots de 1 litre) selon les indications de la page 20.

Couscous algérien de Frédérique

PAR PORTION 1 pot de 500 ml	
Calories	246
Protéines	21 g
M.G.	7 g
Glucides	27 g
Fibres	6 g
Fer	3 mg
Calcium	74 mg
Sodium	249 mg

STÉRILISATION

QUANTITÉ TOTALE • 7 LITRES (28 TASSES)

Taille des pots	Temps de stérilisation
250 ml (8 oz)	65 minutes
500 ml (16 oz)	75 minutes
1 litre (32 oz)	90 minutes

À l'autoclave

Préparation
35 minutes

Trempage
12 heures

Cuisson
9 minutes

- **sans œuf**
- **sans produits laitiers**
- **sans noix**

250 ml (1 tasse) de pois chiches secs (200 g)

30 ml (2 c. à soupe) d'huile végétale

1 kg (environ 2 ¼ lb) d'épaule ou de jarret d'agneau coupé en cubes de 2,5 cm – 1 po

250 ml (1 tasse) d'oignon haché (140 g)

375 ml (1 ½ tasse) de carottes coupées en rondelles (170 g)

1 litre (4 tasses) de navets coupés en dés de 2,5 cm – 1 po (680 g)

750 ml (3 tasses) de courge Butternut coupée en dés de 2,5 cm – 1 po (529 g)

7,5 ml (½ c. à soupe) de cannelle

15 ml (1 c. à soupe) de paprika

5 ml (1 c. à thé) de ras-el-hanout

1 boîte de pâte de tomates de 156 ml

Sel et poivre au goût

3,5 litres (14 tasses) d'eau ou de bouillon au choix (voir recettes aux pages 30, 32 et 40)

250 ml (1 tasse) de pois verts surgelés (120 g)

410 ml (1 ⅔ tasse) de courgettes coupées en rondelles de 1 cm – ½ po (150 g)

750 ml (3 tasses) de chou coupé en tranches de 2,5 cm – 1 po (290 g)

1 boîte de cœurs d'artichauts dans l'eau de 398 ml, égouttés

1. La veille, faire tremper les pois chiches dans 750 ml (3 tasses) d'eau froide de 12 à 18 heures au frais. Le lendemain, égoutter les pois chiches et jeter l'eau de trempage. Rincer les pois chiches à l'eau froide et égoutter de nouveau. Réserver.

2. Dans une grande casserole en acier inoxydable, chauffer l'huile. Faire dorer les cubes d'agneau sur toutes les faces de 2 à 3 minutes.

3. Ajouter l'oignon, les carottes, les navets, la courge, les épices et la pâte de tomates. Saler et poivrer. Ajouter un peu d'huile au besoin. Cuire 2 minutes.

4. Ajouter l'eau (ou le bouillon) et les pois chiches dans la casserole. Porter à ébullition, puis laisser mijoter 5 minutes en remuant pour bien dissoudre la pâte de tomates. Goûter et rectifier l'assaisonnement au besoin.

5. Pendant ce temps, répartir les pois verts, les courgettes, le chou et les cœurs d'artichauts dans les pots.

6. À l'aide d'une cuillère trouée, répartir les aliments solides dans les bocaux, en laissant un espace libre de 2,5 cm (1 po) entre les aliments et le rebord des pots.

7. Verser le bouillon bouillant dans les bocaux, en laissant un espace libre de 2,5 cm (1 po) entre le bouillon et le rebord des pots.

8. Plonger un ustensile dans les pots et le remuer afin d'éliminer toute bulle d'air. Au besoin, ajouter du bouillon.

9. Stériliser à l'autoclave (65 minutes pour des pots de 250 ml, 75 minutes pour des pots de 500 ml et 90 minutes des pots de 1 litre) selon les indications de la page 20.

! Ce plat est tout droit sorti du livre de recettes familiales de Frédérique Trives: il s'agit d'un mets de sa grand-mère Algérienne! On sert la viande et les légumes sur un lit de couscous arrosé du délicieux bouillon.

PAR PORTION 1 pot de 500 ml	
Calories	502
Protéines	42 g
M.G.	27 g
Glucides	24 g
Fibres	6 g
Fer	6 mg
Calcium	88 mg
Sodium	437 mg

Mafé africain

STÉRILISATION

QUANTITÉ TOTALE • 3 LITRES (12 TASSES)

Taille des pots	Temps de stérilisation
250 ml (8 oz)	65 minutes
500 ml (16 oz)	75 minutes
1 litre (32 oz)	90 minutes

À l'autoclave

Préparation
30 minutes

Cuisson
6 minutes

- **sans œuf**
- **sans produits laitiers**
- **sans gluten**

500 ml (2 tasses) de bouillon de bœuf (voir recette à la page 30)

125 ml (½ tasse) de beurre d'arachide non sucré (125 g)

375 ml (1 ½ tasse) de patates douces coupées en dés de 2,5 cm – 1 po (200 g)

375 ml (1 ½ tasse) de carottes coupées en rondelles de 2,5 cm – 1 po (170 g)

45 ml (3 c. à soupe) d'huile végétale ou d'arachide

1 kg (environ 2 ¼ lb) de cubes d'agneau coupés en cubes de 2,5 cm – 1 po

250 ml (1 tasse) d'oignon haché (140 g)

250 ml (1 tasse) de poivron coupé en dés (200 g)

3 gousses d'ail hachées (15 g)

500 ml (2 tasses) de coulis de tomates (voir recette à la page 28)

15 ml (1 c. à soupe) de thym séché

15 ml (1 c. à soupe) de paprika fumé doux

Sel et poivre au goût

1. Dans un bol, fouetter le bouillon avec le beurre d'arachide. Réserver.

2. Répartir les dés de patates douces et les rondelles de carottes dans les pots.

3. Dans une grande casserole en acier inoxydable, chauffer l'huile à feu élevé. Faire dorer les cubes d'agneau sur toutes les faces de 2 à 3 minutes.

4. Répartir les cubes de viande dans les pots.

5. Dans la même casserole, cuire l'oignon et le poivron 3 minutes à feu moyen.

6. Ajouter l'ail et poursuivre la cuisson 1 minute.

7. Ajouter la préparation au beurre d'arachide, le coulis de tomates et les épices dans la casserole. Saler et poivrer. Porter à ébullition.

8. À l'aide d'une cuillère trouée, répartir les aliments solides dans les bocaux, en laissant un espace libre de 2,5 cm (1 po) entre les aliments et le rebord des pots.

9. Verser la sauce bouillante dans les bocaux, en laissant un espace libre de 2,5 cm (1 po) entre la sauce et le rebord des pots.

10. Plonger un ustensile dans les pots et le remuer afin d'éliminer toute bulle d'air. Au besoin, ajouter de la sauce.

11. Stériliser à l'autoclave (65 minutes pour des pots de 250 ml, 75 minutes pour des pots de 500 ml et 90 minutes pour des pots de 1 litre) selon les indications de la page 20.

Viande hachée et à tourtière

PAR PORTION	
1 pot de 500 ml	
Calories	580
Protéines	50 g
M.G.	31 g
Glucides	23 g
Fibres	3 g
Fer	5 mg
Calcium	66 mg
Sodium	965 mg

STÉRILISATION

QUANTITÉ TOTALE • 1 LITRE (4 TASSES)

Taille des pots	Temps de stérilisation
250 ml (8 oz)	65 minutes
500 ml (16 oz)	75 minutes
1 litre (32 oz)	90 minutes

À l'autoclave

Préparation
20 minutes

Cuisson
5 minutes

- **sans œuf**
- **sans produits laitiers**
- **sans noix**
- **sans gluten**

1 lb (450 g) de boeuf haché maigre

180 ml (¾ de tasse) d'oignon haché (100 g)

250 ml (1 tasse) de pomme de terre râpée (180 g)

1 gousse d'ail hachée (5 g)

0,625 ml (⅛ de c. à thé) de cannelle

0,625 ml (⅛ de c. à thé) de clous de girofle moulus

Sel et poivre au goût

500 ml (2 tasses) de bouillon au choix (voir recettes aux pages 30, 32 et 40)

1. Chauffer une grande poêle à feu moyen. Cuire le bœuf et l'oignon de 5 à 7 minutes en égrainant la viande à l'aide d'une cuillère en bois, jusqu'à ce qu'elle ait perdu sa teinte rosée. Environ 1 minute avant la fin de la cuisson, ajouter la pomme de terre, l'ail et les épices dans la poêle. Saler et poivrer.

2. Pendant ce temps, porter le bouillon à ébullition dans une casserole en acier inoxydable.

3. Répartir la préparation à la viande dans les bocaux, en laissant un espace libre de 2,5 cm (1 po) entre la viande et le rebord des pots.

4. Ajouter le bouillon bouillant dans les bocaux, en laissant un espace libre de 2,5 cm (1 po) entre le bouillon et le rebord des pots.

5. Plonger un ustensile dans les pots et le remuer afin d'éliminer toute bulle d'air. Au besoin, ajouter du bouillon.

6. Stériliser à l'autoclave (65 minutes pour des pots de 250 ml, 75 minutes pour des pots de 500 ml et 90 minutes pour des pots de 1 litre) selon les indications de la page 20.

! Au service, il suffit d'ouvrir deux ou trois pots, d'égoutter la préparation, de la verser dans un fond de tarte et de l'enfourner! Comme le gras a tendance à déborder pendant la stérilisation à l'autoclave, je privilégie des coupes de viande maigre. Je vais même égoutter le gras s'il y en a beaucoup. Je vous donne ici la recette pour la viande à tourtières, mais vous pouvez très bien mettre en conserves n'importe quelle viande hachée (porc, poulet, veau, dinde, viande sauvage, etc.) avec la même technique, avec ou sans légumes, changer les épices ou ne pas en ajouter du tout et mettre le bouillon de votre choix.

Sauce à spaghetti de Thérèse

PAR PORTION 1 pot de 1 litre	
Calories	849
Protéines	57 g
M.G.	40 g
Glucides	76 g
Fibres	16 g
Fer	13 mg
Calcium	275 mg
Sodium	3067 mg

STÉRILISATION

QUANTITÉ TOTALE • 7 LITRES (28 TASSES)

Taille des pots	Temps de stérilisation
500 ml (16 oz)	65 minutes
1 litre (32 oz)	75 minutes

À l'autoclave

Préparation
40 minutes

Cuisson
38 minutes

- **sans œuf**
- **sans produits laitiers**
- **sans noix**

3 saucisses italiennes douces (288 g)

680 g (1 ½ lb) de bœuf haché maigre

680 g (1 ½ lb) de porc haché maigre

2 ½ gros oignons coupés en quartiers (375 g)

4 gousses d'ail (20 g)

3 carottes coupées en tronçons (510 g)

4 branches de céleri coupées en tronçons (240 g)

3 courgettes coupées en morceaux (420 g)

1 contenant de champignons de 227 g

2 ½ poivrons rouges coupés en morceaux (450 g)

2 boîtes de jus de tomate de 796 ml chacune

2 boîtes de tomates entières de 796 ml chacune, écrasées avec les mains

1 boîte de tomates broyées de 796 ml

1 boîte de sauce tomate de 680 ml

1 boîte de pâte de tomates de 400 ml

45 ml (3 c. à soupe) de sucre

5 ml (1 c. à thé) de sel de céleri

5 ml (1 c. à thé) de poudre d'ail

5 ml (1 c. à thé) de flocons de piment

5 ml (1 c. à thé) d'origan séché

3 feuilles de laurier émiettées

Sel et poivre au goût

1. Préchauffer le four à 205 °C (400 °F).

2. Retirer les membranes des saucisses et défaire la chair en petits morceaux.

3. Dans une grande poêle, faire dorer le bœuf haché, le porc haché et la chair de saucisses quelques minutes. Égoutter le gras. Transférer la viande cuite dans une grande casserole allant au four.

4. Dans le contenant du robot culinaire, hacher les oignons, l'ail, les carottes et le céleri.

5. Dans la même poêle, cuire les légumes hachés de 6 à 7 minutes à feu moyen. Transférer dans la casserole.

6. Dans le contenant du robot culinaire, hacher les courgettes, les champignons et les poivrons. Transférer dans la casserole.

7. Ajouter le reste des ingrédients dans la casserole. Saler, poivrer et bien mélanger. Cuire au four 30 minutes.

8. Répartir la sauce chaude dans les bocaux, en laissant un espace libre de 2,5 cm (1 po) entre la sauce et le rebord des pots.

9. Plonger un ustensile dans les pots et le remuer afin d'éliminer toute bulle d'air. Au besoin, ajouter de la sauce.

10. Stériliser à l'autoclave (65 minutes pour des pots de 500 ml et 75 minutes pour des pots de 1 litre) selon les indications de la page 20.

! Cette délicieuse recette est celle de mon amie Thérèse Bellemare. Elle la prépare pour ses petits-enfants, qui l'adorent à cause des légumes passés au robot culinaire qu'ils ne voient pas dans la sauce!

Viande sauvage aux champignons

PAR PORTION 1 pot de 500 ml	
Calories	394
Protéines	55 g
M.G.	13 g
Glucides	7 g
Fibres	2 g
Fer	9 mg
Calcium	42 mg
Sodium	425 mg

STÉRILISATION

QUANTITÉ TOTALE • 2 LITRES (8 TASSES)

Taille des pots	Temps de stérilisation
250 ml (8 oz)	65 minutes
500 ml (16 oz)	75 minutes
1 litre (32 oz)	90 minutes

À l'autoclave

Préparation
20 minutes

Cuisson
17 minutes

- sans œuf
- sans produits laitiers
- sans noix
- sans gluten

30 ml (2 c. à soupe) d'huile végétale

900 g (2 lb) de viande sauvage au choix coupée en cubes de 2,5 cm (1 po)

250 ml (1 tasse) d'oignon coupé en demi-rondelles (140 g)

1 contenant de champignons de 227 g, coupés en quatre

2 gousses d'ail hachées (10 g)

125 ml (½ tasse) de vin rouge

375 ml (1 ½ tasse) de bouillon au choix (voir recettes aux pages pages 30, 32 et 40)

15 ml (1 c. à soupe) de romarin séché

1 feuille de laurier émiettée

Sel et poivre au goût

1. Dans une grande poêle, chauffer l'huile à feu moyen. Faire dorer les cubes de viande sur toutes les faces de 4 à 5 minutes.

2. Répartir la viande dans les pots.

3. Dans la même poêle, cuire l'oignon et les champignons 7 minutes à feu moyen.

4. Ajouter l'ail dans la poêle et poursuivre la cuisson 1 minute en remuant.

5. Déglacer avec le vin rouge, en raclant le fond de la poêle avec une cuillère en bois afin de détacher les sucs de cuisson. Laisser réduire 5 minutes.

6. Ajouter le reste des ingrédients et porter à ébullition.

7. À l'aide d'un cuillère trouée, répartir les aliments solides dans les bocaux, en laissant un espace libre de 2,5 cm (1 po) entre les aliments et le rebord des pots.

8. Verser le bouillon bouillant dans les bocaux, en laissant un espace libre de 2,5 cm (1 po) entre le bouillon et le rebord des pots.

9. Plonger un ustensile dans les pots et le remuer afin d'éliminer toute bulle d'air. Au besoin, ajouter du bouillon.

10. Stériliser à l'autoclave (65 minutes pour des pots de 250 ml, 75 minutes pour des pots de 500 ml et 90 minutes pour des pots de 1 litre) selon les indications de la page 20.

! Sachez qu'il est parfaitement sécuritaire de stériliser les viandes sauvages à l'autoclave. N'hésitez donc pas à remplacer n'importe quelle viande de ce livre par celle de votre choix: orignal, cerf, ours, dindon sauvage, etc. On peut épaissir le bouillon au moment de ervir avec un peu de fécule de maïs pour en faire une sauce d'accompagnement.

PAR PORTION 1 pot de 500 ml	
Calories	273
Protéines	26 g
M.G.	11 g
Glucides	18 g
Fibres	4 g
Fer	3 mg
Calcium	85 mg
Sodium	850 mg

Bouilli de bœuf

STÉRILISATION

QUANTITÉ TOTALE • 4,5 LITRES (18 TASSES)

Taille des pots	Temps de stérilisation
250 ml (8 oz)	65 minutes
500 ml (16 oz)	75 minutes
1 litre (32 oz)	90 minutes

À l'autoclave

Préparation
35 minutes

Cuisson
16 minutes

- **sans œuf**
- **sans produits laitiers**
- **sans noix**
- **sans gluten**

1 petit chou coupé en quartiers (290 g)

30 ml (2 c. à soupe) d'huile végétale

900 g (2 lb) de cubes de bœuf à ragoût ou de rôti de bas de palette coupé en cubes de 2,5 cm – 1 po

375 ml (1 ½ tasse) de carottes coupées en rondelles de 1 cm – ½ po (170 g)

250 ml (1 tasse) d'oignon coupé en dés (140 g)

1 petit navet pelé et coupé en dés de 1 cm – ½ po

310 ml (1 ¼ tasse) de pomme de terre Russet ou Yukon Gold pelée et coupée en dés de 1 cm – ½ po

15 ml (1 c. à soupe) de pâte de tomates

2 litres (8 tasses) de bouillon de bœuf (voir recette à la page 30)

60 ml (¼ de tasse) de flocons d'oignon

5 ml (1 c. à thé) de poudre d'oignon

5 ml (1 c. à thé) de poudre d'ail

5 ml (1 c. à thé) de persil séché

0,625 ml (⅛ de c. à thé) de grains de céleri

1 feuille de laurier émiettée

Sel et poivre au goût

1. Répartir les quartiers de chou dans les pots.

2. Dans une grande casserole en acier inoxydable, chauffer l'huile à feu élevé. Faire dorer les cubes de bœuf sur toutes les faces de 4 à 5 minutes.

3. Ajouter les légumes et la pâte de tomates dans la casserole. Remuer et poursuivre la cuisson 7 minutes à feu moyen-élevé.

4. Déglacer avec le bouillon, en raclant le fond de la casserole avec une cuillère en bois afin de détacher les sucs de cuisson. Ajouter les épices. Saler et poivrer. Porter à ébullition, puis laisser mijoter 5 minutes. Goûter et rectifier l'assaisonnement au besoin.

5. À l'aide d'une cuillère trouée, répartir les aliments solides dans les bocaux, en laissant un espace libre de 2,5 cm (1 po) entre les aliments et le rebord des pots.

6. Verser le bouillon bouillant dans les bocaux, en laissant un espace libre de 2,5 cm (1 po) entre le bouillon et le rebord des pots.

7. Plonger un ustensile dans les pots et le remuer afin d'éliminer toute bulle d'air. Au besoin, ajouter du bouillon.

8. Stériliser à l'autoclave (65 minutes pour des pots de 250 ml, 75 minutes pour des pots de 500 ml et 90 minutes pour des pots de 1 litre) selon les indications de la page 20.

! Un classique québécois! Il existe autant de variantes de cette recette qu'il y a de familles. Certains mettent en conserve tous les ingrédients crus, mais je préfère faire dorer certains ingrédients avant d'empoter pour ajouter de la saveur. Attention: le goût du chou et du navet stérilisés à l'autoclave est très fort et ne plaît pas à tous. Faites de petites quantités de cette recette avant de vous lancer dans une grande production!

PAR PORTION 1 pot de 500 ml	
Calories	532
Protéines	40 g
M.G.	29 g
Glucides	33 g
Fibres	7 g
Fer	6 mg
Calcium	101 mg
Sodium	273 mg

Boulettes de veau

STÉRILISATION

QUANTITÉ TOTALE • 2 LITRES (8 TASSES)

Taille des pots	Temps de stérilisation
250 ml (8 oz)	65 minutes
500 ml (16 oz)	75 minutes
1 litre (32 oz)	90 minutes

À l'autoclave

Préparation
30 minutes

Temps de repos
10 minutes

Cuisson
12 minutes

- **sans produits laitiers**
- **sans noix**

Pour les boulettes :

125 ml (½ tasse) de son d'avoine (60 g)

60 ml (¼ de tasse) d'eau bouillante

700 g (environ 1 ½ lb) de veau haché

1 œuf battu

15 ml (1 c. à soupe) d'assaisonnements italiens

Pour la sauce :

15 ml (1 c. à soupe) d'huile végétale

80 ml (⅓ de tasse) de céleri haché finement (40 g)

250 ml (1 tasse) d'oignon haché finement (140 g)

180 ml (¾ de tasse) de carotte hachée (120 g)

310 ml (1 ⅓ tasse) de poivron haché (185 g)

2 gousses d'ail hachées (10 g)

1 litre (4 tasses) de coulis de tomates (voir recette à la page 28)

Sel et poivre au goût

1. Dans un petit bol, mélanger le son d'avoine avec l'eau bouillante. Laisser gonfler 10 minutes.

2. Préchauffer le four à 260 °C (500 °F).

3. Dans un grand bol, déposer la préparation au son d'avoine et le reste des ingrédients des boulettes. Bien mélanger.

4. Façonner des boulettes de 2,5 cm (1 po) de diamètre et les déposer sur une plaque de cuisson tapissée de papier parchemin. Cuire au four 10 minutes.

5. Pendant ce temps, chauffer l'huile à feu moyen-élevé dans une grande casserole en acier inoxydable. Cuire les légumes environ 7 minutes.

6. Ajouter le coulis de tomates dans la casserole. Saler et poivrer. Porter à ébullition, puis laisser mijoter 5 minutes.

7. Répartir les boulettes dans les bocaux, en laissant un espace libre de 3,5 cm (1 ½ po) entre les boulettes et le rebord des pots.

8. Verser la sauce bouillante dans les bocaux, en laissant un espace libre de 2,5 cm (1 po) entre la sauce et le rebord des pots.

9. Plonger un ustensile dans les pots et le remuer afin d'éliminer toute bulle d'air. Au besoin, ajouter de la sauce.

10. Stériliser à l'autoclave (65 minutes pour des pots de 250 ml, 75 minutes pour des pots de 500 ml et 90 minutes pour des pots de 1 litre) selon les indications de la page 20.

VÉGÉ

Grande oubliée des livres de conserves pendant plusieurs décennies, la cuisine végé s'adapte pourtant très bien à la mise en pots. Je vous propose un tour du monde des saveurs avec des recettes bourrées de légumineuses, dont le Canada est l'un des plus importants producteurs mondiaux.

Caponata

PAR PORTION 1 pot de 250 ml	
Calories	99
Protéines	2 g
M.G.	6 g
Glucides	10 g
Fibres	3 g
Fer	1 mg
Calcium	39 mg
Sodium	154 mg

STÉRILISATION

QUANTITÉ TOTALE • 1 LITRE (4 TASSES)

Taille des pots	Temps de stérilisation
125 ml (4 oz)	15 minutes
250 ml (8 oz)	15 minutes
500 ml (16 oz)	15 minutes
1 litre (32 oz)	15 minutes

À la casserole

Préparation
15 minutes

Cuisson
25 minutes

- **sans œuf**
- **sans produits laitiers**
- **sans noix**
- **végé**
- **sans gluten**

22,5 ml (1 ½ c. à soupe) d'huile végétale

60 ml (¼ de tasse) de céleri coupé en dés (35 g)

125 ml (½ tasse) d'oignon coupé en dés (70 g)

125 ml (½ tasse) de poivron rouge coupé en dés (100 g)

180 ml (¾ de tasse) de courgette coupée en dés (100 g)

250 ml (1 tasse) d'aubergine coupée en dés (92 g)

1 gousse d'ail hachée (5 g)

15 ml (1 c. à soupe) de vinaigre de vin rouge à 5 % d'acide acétique

2,5 ml (½ c. à thé) de vinaigre balsamique à 6 % d'acide acétique

15 ml (1 c. à soupe) de jus de citron en bouteille

625 ml (2 ½ tasses) de tomates en dés ou de coulis de tomates (voir recette à la page 28)

30 ml (2 c. à soupe) de petites olives vertes farcies

30 ml (2 c. à soupe) de câpres marinées

2,5 ml (½ c. à thé) de flocons de piment (facultatif)

30 ml (2 c. à soupe) de persil frais haché (5 g)

5 ml (1 c. à thé) de basilic séché

5 ml (1 c. à thé) d'origan séché

1 pincée de sucre (facultatif)

Sel et poivre au goût (attention, les câpres et les olives sont déjà salées)

1. Dans une grande poêle à haut rebord, chauffer l'huile à feu moyen.

2. Cuire le céleri, l'oignon, le poivron, la courgette, l'aubergine et l'ail 10 minutes.

3. Déglacer avec les vinaigres et le jus de citron, en raclant le fond de la poêle avec une cuillère en bois afin de détacher les sucs de cuisson.

4. Ajouter le reste des ingrédients dans la poêle et laisser mijoter de 15 à 20 minutes à feu doux-moyen.

5. Répartir la caponata bouillante dans les bocaux, en laissant un espace libre de 1 cm (½ po) entre la préparation et le rebord des pots.

6. Plonger un ustensile dans les pots et le remuer afin d'éliminer toute bulle d'air. Au besoin, ajouter de la préparation.

7. Stériliser à la casserole 15 minutes (pour les pots de 125 ml, de 250 ml, de 500 ml ou de 1 litre) selon les indications de la page 19.

La caponata est la version italienne de la ratatouille, mais elle est un peu plus goûteuse. Je sers cette recette autant froide (en antipasto ou en bruschetta) que chaude (en garniture sur des pâtes). Ma façon préférée de la servir est de la réchauffer dans une grande poêle, d'y casser des œufs, d'ajouter un peu de fromage râpé et d'enfourner le tout, juste le temps que les œufs cuisent. Je déguste ensuite la caponata avec du bon pain, comme le font les Italiens (ils appellent cela «*fare la scarpetta*»). Il est important ici de bien respecter la liste d'ingrédients et les proportions, puisque le pH a été spécifiquement testé pour que la recette puisse être cannée à la casserole (donc sans autoclave!).

PAR PORTION 1 pot de 500 ml	
Calories	322
Protéines	12 g
M.G.	8 g
Glucides	54 g
Fibres	11 g
Fer	4 mg
Calcium	104 mg
Sodium	266 mg

Tajine aux légumes

STÉRILISATION

QUANTITÉ TOTALE • 2,5 LITRES (10 TASSES)

Taille des pots	Temps de stérilisation
500 ml (16 oz)	65 minutes
1 litre (32 oz)	75 minutes

À l'autoclave

Préparation
30 minutes

Trempage
12 heures

Cuisson
23 minutes

- sans œuf
- sans produits laitiers
- sans noix
- végé
- sans gluten

125 ml (½ tasse) de pois chiches secs (85 g)

30 ml (2 c. à soupe) d'huile végétale

250 ml (1 tasse) d'oignon coupé en dés (140 g)

½ contenant de champignons blancs de 227 g, coupés en quartiers

375 ml (1 ½ tasse) de courgettes coupées en demi-rondelles de 2,5 cm – 1 po (200 g)

250 ml (1 tasse) de céleri émincé (140 g)

560 ml (2 ¼ tasses) de poivrons coupés en dés (450 g)

250 ml (1 tasse) de carottes coupées en rondelles de 2,5 cm – 1 po (140 g)

2 gousses d'ail hachées (10 g)

15 ml (1 c. à soupe) de mélange d'épices à couscous (voir encadré ci-dessous)

30 ml (2 c. à soupe) de harissa

1 litre (4 tasses) de coulis de tomates (voir recette à la page 28)

250 ml (1 tasse) de bouillon de légumes (voir recette à la page 32)

250 ml (1 tasse) de pomme de terre Russet ou Yukon Gold rincée et coupée en dés de 2,5 cm – 1 po (200 g)

250 ml (1 tasse) de patate douce pelée et coupée en dés de 1 cm – ½ po (175 g)

Sel et poivre au goût

1. La veille, faire tremper les pois chiches dans 375 ml (1 ½ tasse) d'eau froide de 12 à 18 heures au frais. Le lendemain, jeter l'eau de trempage, puis rincer et égoutter les pois chiches. Réserver.

2. Dans une grande casserole en acier inoxydable, chauffer l'huile à feu élevé. Cuire l'oignon, les champignons, les courgettes, le céleri, les poivrons et les carottes 7 minutes en remuant.

3. Ajouter l'ail, les épices à couscous et la harissa dans la casserole. Poursuivre la cuisson 1 minute.

4. Ajouter les pois chiches et le reste des ingrédients, puis laisser mijoter 15 minutes à feu doux-moyen, en remuant de temps en temps. Goûter et rectifier l'assaisonnement au besoin.

5. À l'aide d'une cuillère trouée, répartir le mélange de pois chiches et légumes dans les bocaux, en laissant un espace libre de 3,5 cm (1 ½ po) entre la préparation et le rebord des pots.

6. Verser la sauce bouillante dans les bocaux, en laissant un espace libre de 2,5 cm (1 po) entre la sauce et le rebord des pots.

7. Plonger un ustensile dans les pots et le remuer afin d'éliminer toute bulle d'air. Au besoin, ajouter de la sauce.

8. Stériliser à l'autoclave (65 minutes pour des pots de 500 ml et 75 minutes pour des pots de 1 litre) selon les indications de la page 20.

Ma recette de mélange d'épices à couscous

Dans un bol, mélanger 45 ml (3 c. à soupe) de cumin avec 30 ml (2 c. à soupe) de sel, 15 ml (1 c. à soupe) chacun de poivre noir moulu, de cannelle, de piment de Cayenne et de grains de coriandre moulus, et 10 ml (2 c. à thé) chacun de clous de girofle moulus, de paprika et de curcuma.

Sauce pour pâtes à l'aubergine

PAR PORTION 1 pot de 500 ml	
Calories	261
Protéines	5 g
M.G.	11 g
Glucides	28 g
Fibres	8 g
Fer	3 mg
Calcium	76 mg
Sodium	53 mg

STÉRILISATION

QUANTITÉ TOTALE • 1 LITRE (4 TASSES)

Taille des pots	Temps de stérilisation
500 ml (16 oz)	30 minutes
1 litre (32 oz)	40 minutes

Préparation
5 minutes

Cuisson
45 minutes

- **sans œuf**
- **sans produits laitiers**
- **sans noix**
- **végé**
- **sans gluten**

500 ml (2 tasses) d'aubergine coupée en dés de 2,5 cm – 1 po (200 g)

250 ml (1 tasse) d'oignon coupé en dés (140 g)

2 gousses d'ail hachées (10 g)

22,5 ml (1 ½ c. à soupe) d'huile d'olive

Sel et poivre au goût

500 ml (2 tasses) de coulis de tomates (voir recette à la page 28) ou de tomates en dés

125 ml (½ tasse) de vin rouge

30 ml (2 c. à soupe) de basilic frais haché grossièrement

15 ml (1 c. à soupe) de persil frais haché grossièrement

2,5 ml (½ c. à thé) de flocons de piment (facultatif)

1 pincée de sucre (facultatif)

0,625 ml (⅛ de c. à thé) de fumée liquide (facultatif, mais très bon)

1. Préchauffer le four à 205 °C (400 °F).

2. Sur une grande plaque de cuisson ou dans un plat de cuisson, déposer l'aubergine, l'oignon et l'ail. Arroser d'huile, puis saler, poivrer et remuer. Cuire au four 30 minutes.

3. Pendant ce temps, verser le coulis de tomates dans une grande casserole en acier inoxydable. Laisser mijoter à feu doux en remuant de temps en temps, jusqu'à ce que le coulis ait légèrement réduit.

4. Ajouter l'aubergine, l'oignon et l'ail cuits dans la casserole.

5. Déglacer la plaque de cuisson avec le vin, en raclant le fond avec une cuillère en bois afin de détacher les sucs de cuisson. Transvider la préparation au vin dans la casserole.

6. Ajouter le reste des ingrédients dans la casserole et laisser mijoter 15 minutes à feu doux-moyen, en remuant de temps en temps. Goûter et rectifier l'assaisonnement au besoin.

7. Répartir la sauce bouillante dans les bocaux, en laissant un espace libre de 2,5 cm (1 po) entre la sauce et le rebord des pots.

8. Plonger un ustensile dans les pots et le remuer afin d'éliminer toute bulle d'air. Au besoin, ajouter de la sauce.

9. Stériliser à l'autoclave (30 minutes pour des pots de 500 ml et 40 minutes pour des pots de 1 litre) selon les indications de la page 20.

Sauce à spaghetti aux lentilles

PAR PORTION 1 pot de 500 ml	
Calories	197
Protéines	8 g
M.G.	6 g
Glucides	32 g
Fibres	8 g
Fer	4 mg
Calcium	85 mg
Sodium	416 mg

STÉRILISATION

QUANTITÉ TOTALE • 3 LITRES (12 TASSES)

Taille des pots	Temps de stérilisation
500 ml (16 oz)	65 minutes
1 litre (32 oz)	75 minutes

À l'autoclave

Préparation
30 minutes

Cuisson
20 minutes

- **sans œuf**
- **sans produits laitiers**
- **sans noix**
- **végé**
- **sans gluten**

30 ml (2 c. à soupe) d'huile végétale

500 ml (2 tasses) de poivrons coupés en dés (400 g)

500 ml (2 tasses) de carottes coupées en dés (280 g)

375 ml (1 ½ tasse) de céleri coupé en dés (210 g)

1 contenant de champignons blancs de 227 g, coupés en dés

250 ml (1 tasse) d'oignon coupé en dés (140 g)

1 litre (4 tasses) de coulis de tomates (voir recette à la page 28)

500 ml (2 tasses) de bouillon de légumes (voir recette à la page 32)

250 ml (1 tasse) de lentilles brunes rincées et égouttées (250 g)

15 ml (1 c. à soupe) de sauce Worcestershire

15 ml (1 c. à soupe) d'herbes italiennes séchées

2 gousses d'ail hachées (10 g)

1 feuille de laurier émiettée

1 piment thaï (5 g) haché (facultatif)

Sel et poivre au goût

1. Dans une grande casserole en acier inoxydable, chauffer l'huile à feu élevé. Cuire les légumes de 5 à 7 minutes en remuant.

2. Ajouter le reste des ingrédients dans la casserole et laisser mijoter 15 minutes à feu doux-moyen, en remuant de temps en temps. Goûter et rectifier l'assaisonnement au besoin.

3. Répartir la sauce bouillante dans les bocaux, en laissant un espace libre de 2,5 cm (1 po) entre la sauce et le rebord des pots.

4. Plonger un ustensile dans les pots et le remuer afin d'éliminer toute bulle d'air. Au besoin, ajouter de la sauce.

5. Stériliser à l'autoclave (65 minutes pour des pots de 500 ml et 75 minutes pour des pots de 1 litre) selon les indications de la page 20.

! La sauce semblera trop liquide au moment d'empoter, et c'est normal. Les lentilles vont absorber le liquide et épaissir la sauce lors de la stérilisation dans l'autoclave.

PAR PORTION 1 pot de 500 ml	
Calories	549
Protéines	26 g
M.G.	16 g
Glucides	80 g
Fibres	11 g
Fer	9 mg
Calcium	100 mg
Sodium	865 mg

Dahl indien de mon frère Max

STÉRILISATION

QUANTITÉ TOTALE • 1,5 LITRE (6 TASSES)

Taille des pots	Temps de stérilisation
500 ml (16 oz)	65 minutes
1 litre (32 oz)	75 minutes

Préparation
10 minutes

Cuisson
10 minutes

- **sans œuf**
- **sans produits laitiers**
- **sans noix**
- **végé**
- **sans gluten**

375 ml (1 ½ tasse) de pois cassés jaunes (300 g)

45 ml (3 c. à soupe) d'huile végétale

30 ml (2 c. à soupe) de curcuma

5 ml (1 c. à thé) de grains de cumin

5 ml (1 c. à thé) de grains de moutarde

5 ml (1 c. à thé) de flocons de piment (facultatif)

2,5 ml (½ c. à thé) de coriandre moulue

2,5 ml (½ c. à thé) de garam masala

2,5 ml (½ c. à thé) de poudre de cari

2,5 ml (½ c. à thé) de poudre d'oignon

2,5 ml (½ c. à thé) de poivre noir fraîchement moulu

2 gousses d'ail hachées (10 g)

7,5 ml (½ c. à soupe) de gingembre haché (8 g)

250 ml (1 tasse) d'oignon haché (140 g)

180 ml (¾ de tasse) de tomates (fraîches ou en conserve) hachées (200 g)

1 litre (4 tasses) d'eau ou de bouillon de légumes (voir recette à la page 32)

Sel au goût

1. À l'aide d'une passoire fine, rincer les pois cassés à l'eau froide. Égoutter.

2. Répartir les pois cassés dans les pots.

3. Dans une grande poêle, chauffer l'huile à feu doux-moyen. Cuire les épices de 3 à 4 minutes.

4. Ajouter l'ail et le gingembre dans la poêle. Poursuivre la cuisson 2 minutes.

5. Ajouter l'oignon et les tomates. Poursuivre la cuisson 5 minutes.

6. Ajouter l'eau ou le bouillon de légumes et porter à ébullition. Goûter et rectifier l'assaisonnement au besoin.

7. Répartir la préparation aux épices bouillante dans les bocaux, en laissant un espace libre de 2,5 cm (1 po) entre la préparation et le rebord des pots.

8. Plonger un ustensile dans les pots et le remuer afin d'éliminer toute bulle d'air. Au besoin, ajouter de la préparation.

9. Stériliser à l'autoclave (65 minutes pour des pots de 500 ml et 75 minutes pour des pots de 1 litre) selon les indications de la page 20.

Mon frère Maxime a eu la chance de passer six semaines en Inde, et il a rapporté cette authentique et délicieuse recette remplie de parfums indiens. On la sert sur un lit de riz avec des échalotes frites, du yogourt nature et de la coriandre fraîche.

Salade de légumineuses

PAR PORTION 1 pot de 500 ml	
Calories	739
Protéines	11 g
M.G.	59 g
Glucides	31 g
Fibres	9 g
Fer	3 mg
Calcium	85 mg
Sodium	1064 mg

STÉRILISATION

QUANTITÉ TOTALE • 2 LITRES (8 TASSES)

Taille des pots	Temps de stérilisation
125 ml (4 oz)	15 minutes
250 ml (8 oz)	15 minutes
500 ml (16 oz)	15 minutes
1 litre (32 oz)	15 minutes

À la casserole

Préparation
25 minutes

Trempage
12 heures

Cuisson
1 heure 2 minutes

Temps de repos
1 heure

- **sans œuf**
- **sans produits laitiers**
- **sans noix**
- **végé**
- **sans gluten**

125 ml (½ tasse) de haricots romains secs (90 g)

125 ml (½ tasse) de haricots mungo secs (100 g)

500 ml (2 tasses) d'eau

250 ml (1 tasse) de vinaigre blanc à 5 % d'acide acétique

250 ml (1 tasse) de jus de citron en bouteille

250 ml (1 tasse) d'huile végétale

7,5 ml (½ c. à soupe) de sel

250 ml (1 tasse) de céleri coupé en dés (140 g)

250 ml (1 tasse) de chou-fleur coupé en petits bouquets (120 g)

250 ml (1 tasse) de poivrons de couleurs variées coupés en dés (200 g)

125 ml (½ tasse) d'oignon haché (70 g)

1 jalapeño (50 g) épépiné et coupé en dés (facultatif)

1. La veille, bien rincer les haricots à l'eau froide à l'aide d'une passoire fine. Déposer séparément les haricots dans deux grands bols remplis de 500 ml (2 tasses) d'eau froide chacun. Laisser tremper au frais toute une nuit (de 12 à 18 heures).

2. Au moment de la cuisson, égoutter les haricots et jeter l'eau de trempage. Rincer de nouveau les haricots à l'eau froide. Égoutter.

3. Dans deux casseroles en acier inoxydable, déposer séparément les haricots. Couvrir d'eau froide et cuire environ 1 heure à feu doux, jusqu'à tendreté. Égoutter.

4. Dans une troisième casserole en acier inoxydable, mélanger l'eau avec le vinaigre, le jus de citron, l'huile et le sel. Porter à ébullition.

5. Ajouter les haricots cuits et les légumes dans la casserole. Porter à ébullition et laisser mijoter 2 minutes à feu doux-moyen.

6. Éteindre le feu et laisser reposer 1 heure en remuant régulièrement. Porter à ébullition de nouveau.

7. À l'aide d'une cuillère trouée, répartir la préparation aux haricots dans les bocaux, en laissant un espace libre de 1 cm (½ po) entre la préparation et le rebord des pots.

8. Ajouter le liquide bouillant dans les bocaux, en laissant un espace libre de 0,5 cm (¼ de po) entre le liquide et le rebord des pots.

9. Plonger un ustensile dans les pots et le remuer afin d'éliminer toute bulle d'air. Au besoin, ajouter du liquide.

10. Stériliser à la casserole 15 minutes (pour des pots de 125 ml, de 250 ml, de 500 ml ou de 1 litre) selon les indications de la page 19.

! Pour cette recette, on cuit les haricots séparément pour qu'ils gardent leur couleur. On peut ajouter un peu de sucre à l'étape 4 pour adoucir le goût du vinaigre. D'ailleurs, cette salade fait un excellent lunch! J'aime bien y ajouter un peu de feta émiettée au moment de servir.

Chana masala aux pois chiches

PAR PORTION 1 pot de 500 ml	
Calories	631
Protéines	25 g
M.G.	21 g
Glucides	92 g
Fibres	15 g
Fer	8 mg
Calcium	140 mg
Sodium	204 mg

STÉRILISATION

QUANTITÉ TOTALE • 2 LITRES (8 TASSES)

Taille des pots	Temps de stérilisation
500 ml (16 oz)	65 minutes
1 litre (32 oz)	75 minutes

À l'autoclave

Préparation
10 minutes

Trempage
12 heures

Cuisson
16 minutes

- sans œuf
- sans produits laitiers
- sans noix
- végé
- sans gluten

500 ml (2 tasses) de pois chiches secs (400 g)

60 ml (¼ de tasse) d'huile végétale

2 feuilles de laurier émiettées

22,5 ml (1 ½ c. à soupe) de coriandre moulue

7,5 ml (½ c. à soupe) de grains de cumin

7,5 ml (½ c. à soupe) de garam masala

7,5 ml (½ c. à soupe) de fenugrec (facultatif)

5 ml (1 c. à thé) de cumin

5 ml (1 c. à thé) de poudre de chili (facultatif)

2,5 ml (½ c. à thé) de curcuma

2,5 ml (½ c. à thé) de poivre noir fraîchement moulu

3 gousses d'ail hachées (15 g)

15 ml (1 c. à soupe) de gingembre haché (12 g)

160 ml (⅔ de tasse) de poivron ou de piment fort au choix coupé en dés (135 g)

750 ml (3 tasses) d'oignons hachés (420 g)

375 ml (1 ½ tasse) de tomates (fraîches ou en conserve) broyées (325 g)

500 ml (2 tasses) d'eau

15 ml (1 c. à soupe) de sucre (facultatif)

Sel au goût

1. La veille, rincer les pois chiches à l'eau froide à l'aide d'une passoire fine. Déposer les pois chiches dans un grand bol rempli de 1,5 litre (6 tasses) d'eau froide. Laisser tremper au frais toute une nuit (de 12 à 18 heures).

2. Au moment de la cuisson, égoutter les pois chiches et jeter l'eau de trempage. Rincer de nouveau les pois chiches à l'eau froide et égoutter. Réserver.

3. Dans une grande poêle, chauffer l'huile à feu doux-moyen. Cuire les épices de 3 à 4 minutes.

4. Ajouter l'ail, le gingembre et le poivron ou le piment dans la poêle. Poursuivre la cuisson 3 minutes.

5. Ajouter les oignons et les tomates. Poursuivre la cuisson 5 minutes.

6. Ajouter l'eau et le sucre, puis porter à ébullition. Goûter et rectifier l'assaisonnement au besoin.

7. Si désiré, réduire la préparation en purée à l'aide du mélangeur à main, jusqu'à l'obtention d'une texture lisse. Ajouter les pois chiches dans la casserole et poursuivre la cuisson 5 minutes à feu moyen.

8. Répartir la préparation aux pois chiches bouillante dans les bocaux, en laissant un espace libre de 2,5 cm (1 po) entre la préparation et le rebord des pots.

9. Plonger un ustensile dans les pots et le remuer afin d'éliminer toute bulle d'air. Au besoin, ajouter de la préparation.

10. Stériliser à l'autoclave (65 minutes pour des pots de 500 ml et 75 minutes pour des pots de 1 litre) selon les indications de la page 20.

Au moment du repas, vous pouvez réchauffer ce plat et y ajouter du yogourt ou de la crème pour un goût bien riche. À servir avec du riz et un peu de coriandre fraîche.

Chili végé aux patates douces de Karine

PAR PORTION 1 pot de 500 ml	
Calories	219
Protéines	11 g
M.G.	5 g
Glucides	39 g
Fibres	9 g
Fer	5 mg
Calcium	122 mg
Sodium	416 mg

STÉRILISATION

QUANTITÉ TOTALE • 8 LITRES (32 TASSES)

Taille des pots	Temps de stérilisation
500 ml (16 oz)	65 minutes
1 litre (32 oz)	75 minutes

À l'autoclave

Préparation
30 minutes

Trempage
12 heures

Cuisson
10 minutes

- sans œuf
- sans produits laitiers
- sans noix
- végé
- sans gluten

1 sac de haricots pinto secs de 900 g

30 ml (2 c. à soupe) d'huile végétale

750 ml (3 tasses) d'oignons hachés (420 g)

500 ml (2 tasses) de poivrons rouges coupés en dés (400 g)

6 gousses d'ail hachées (30 g)

4 litres (16 tasses) de coulis de tomates (voir recette à la page 28) ou de tomates broyées

2 litres (8 tasses) d'eau ou de bouillon de légumes (voir recette à la page 32)

1 litre (4 tasses) de patates douces coupées en cubes de 1 cm – ½ pouce (350 g)

930 ml (3 ¾ tasses) d'edamames décortiqués surgelés (500 g)

750 ml (3 tasses) de mélange de haricots verts et jaunes surgelés (375 g)

250 ml (1 tasse) de maïs surgelé (140 g)

45 ml (3 c. à soupe) de mélange d'épices mexicain (voir recette à la page 44)

30 ml (2 c. à soupe) de mélasse (facultatif)

Sel et poivre au goût

1. La veille, rincer les haricots à l'eau froide à l'aide d'une passoire fine. Déposer les haricots dans un très grand bol rempli de 2,5 litres (10 tasses) d'eau froide. Laisser tremper au frais toute une nuit (de 12 à 18 heures).

2. Au moment de la cuisson, égoutter les haricots et jeter l'eau de trempage. Rincer de nouveau les haricots à l'eau froide et égoutter. Réserver.

3. Dans une grande casserole en acier inoxydable, chauffer l'huile à feu moyen. Cuire les oignons, les poivrons et l'ail 5 minutes.

4. Ajouter les haricots et le reste des ingrédients dans la casserole. Porter à ébullition et laisser mijoter 5 minutes à feu doux-moyen.

5. Répartir le chili bouillant dans les bocaux, en laissant un espace libre de 2,5 cm (1 po) entre le chili et le rebord des pots.

6. Plonger un ustensile dans les pots et le remuer afin d'éliminer toute bulle d'air. Au besoin, ajouter du chili.

7. Stériliser à l'autoclave (65 minutes pour des pots de 500 ml et 75 minutes pour des pots de 1 litre) selon les indications de la page 20.

Vous avez oublié de faire tremper les haricots pinto la veille? Pas de problème! Déposez-les dans une casserole avec 3 fois leur volume en eau, portez le tout à ébullition et laissez mijoter 2 minutes, puis éteignez le feu. Laissez ensuite gonfler les haricots pendant 1 heure, et voilà!

!

Cette recette provient de Karine Damphousse, qui était d'abord une cliente et qui est maintenant une amie. Végétarienne depuis plus de 16 ans, elle m'a souvent demandé de faire des recettes sans viande pouvant être mises en conserves, et j'aimerais la remercier d'avoir insisté: j'ai ainsi découvert un tas de belles recettes végé! Cette recette-ci a un goût assez doux qui plaira aux enfants, mais n'hésitez pas à y ajouter plus d'épices pour un chili plus goûteux ou piquant!

INDEX DES RECETTES

Soupes et potages

PRATICO
EDITION